Multiple Choice Questions
related to the

OXFORD TEXTBOOK OF MEDICINE

THIRD EDITION

Richard Hawkins MBBS FRCS

PASTEST

Multiple Choice Questions
related to the

OXFORD
TEXTBOOK OF
MEDICINE

THIRD EDITION

Richard Hawkins MBBS FRCS

First published 1983
Second Edition 1987
Third Edition 1996

A catalogue record for this publication is available from the British Library.

ISBN 0 906896 48 7

Typeset by EDITEXT, Knutsford, Cheshire.
Printed by Hobbs the Printers Limited, Totton, Hampshire.

iv

CONTENTS

Each section listed below contains questions based on the corresponding section in the *Oxford Textbook of Medicine*, Third Edition.

(Note: brackets indicate the number of questions in each section.)

ACKNOWLEDGEMENTS

Dr Gareth Holsgrove BEd MSc PhD, Senior Lecturer in Medical Education, St Bartholomew's and the Royal London Hospitals School of Medicine and Dentistry.

Dr Phil Kalra MA MB MRCP, Consultant Nephrologist, Hope Hospital, Salford.

Dr Charles J Knight MA MRCP, Clinical Research Fellow, Royal Brompton Hospital, London.

Dr Sam Lim FRACP, Senior Clinical Research Fellow, Royal Brompton National Heart and Lung Hospital, London.

Dr Christopher E G Moore BSc MB BS MRCP, MRC Training Fellow and Honorary Senior Registrar, Manchester Royal Infirmary.

Dr Deven J Patel MB MRCP, Clinical Research Fellow, Royal Brompton Hospital, London.

Dr Paul Strickland BSc MB ChB MMedSc MRCPsych, Clinical Research Fellow and Honorary Senior Registrar, University Hospital of South Manchester.

Dr Anne Yardumian MD MRCP MRCPath, Consultant Haematologist, North Middlesex Hospital.

Grateful thanks are also due to the many specialists who have read the questions in this book and have offered their invaluable advice.

INTRODUCTION

This PASTEST revision book contains over 370 multiple choice questions related to the *Oxford Textbook of Medicine*, Oxford University Press, Third Edition, 1995, edited by D. J. Weatherall, J. G. G. Ledingham and D. A. Warrell. The questions presented cover all the main subject headings.

Every effort has been made to ensure that the *Oxford Textbook of Medicine* is of value not only to physicians practising in developed countries but also to those in other parts of the world. For this reason there is extensive coverage of infectious and tropical diseases.

This PASTEST MCQ book will be an invaluable revision aid to all doctors studying for professional qualifications. The multiple choice questions are particularly relevant to doctors studying for the MRCP Part 1 examination. They have been designed to be similar in style, content and level of difficulty to those used in the Royal College of Physicians examination.

Each question consists of an initial statement (or 'stem') followed by five possible completions (or 'items') identified by A B C D E. There is no restriction on the number of true or false items in a question. It is possible for all the items in a question to be true, or for all to be false.

The answers to each question are to be found at the end of this book, together with a specific page reference to the *Oxford Textbook of Medicine*, Third Edition. The student, having studied and answered the multiple choice questions in one section, can then check his answers and learn from his mistakes by turning to the specific pages referred to in the *Oxford Textbook of Medicine*. In this way a systematic method of revision can be achieved without attempting the daunting task of reading an entire section of the *Textbook* at a time! In this Third Edition, we have included concise explanatory notes for every question. This enables the user to work with or without reference to the *Textbook*.

PASTEST REVISION BOOKS AND COURSES

PasTest has been established in the field of postgraduate medical education since 1972, providing revision books, practice exams and intensive revision courses for doctors preparing for professional examinations.

PasTest Intensive Revision Courses are run before each examination at convenient locations in major cities. All courses offer top quality revision materials and expert teaching.

PasTest Practice Exams and Revision Books are available for MRCP Parts 1 & 2 (General Medicine, Paediatric & Clinical), MRCGP, DRCOG, MRCOG, DCH, FRCS, FRCA, PLAB & undergraduate finals.

SECTION 5: IMMUNE MECHANISMS IN HEALTH AND DISEASE

Indicate your answers with a tick or a cross against each answer option. The answers and teaching notes start on page 115.

5.1   Mast cells

    A   are derived from monocytes
    B   act as a potent activator of natural killer cells
    C   release leukotrienes
    D   can differentiate to become T-cells
    E   are responsible for the anaphylactic type of allergic reaction

5.2 H_1-receptors are responsible for

    A   hypersecretion of mucus
    B   pruritus
    C   gastric acid secretion
    D   contraction of non-vascular smooth muscle
    E   relaxation of vascular smooth muscle

5.3   The recognized clinical features of anaphylaxis include

    A   facial pallor
    B   hypertension
    C   arrhythmias
    D   urinary incontinence
    E   bronchodilatation

5.4   Allergic rhinitis

    A   affects about 1 in 10 people in Western countries
    B   follows IgG-mediated degranulation of mast cells and basophils
    C   occurs equally in all generations
    D   is often accompanied by nasal polyps
    E   occurs usually in families with a history of atopy

5.5 Desensitization (allergen immunotherapy)

A has been used for IgE-mediated disorders since the early 20th century

B involves the subcutaneous injection of ever decreasing doses of soluble allergen extract as the patient's tolerance develops

C should not be used in combination with drugs

D should not be performed unless full resuscitation facilities are available

E has been shown in controlled studies to have a significant placebo effect

5.6 Desensitization is appropriate treatment for the following conditions:

A asthma

B bee venom hypersensitivity

C house-dust mite allergen hypersensitivity

D severe summer hayfever

E tree pollen hypersensitivity

5.7 Common varied immunodeficiency (common varied hypogamma globulinaemia)

A typically presents in early childhood

B typically causes serum IgM levels to be very low

C causes severe lymphopenia in about a third of patients

D causes death from opportunistic fungal and viral infections in most patients within five years of diagnosis

E causes patients to be particularly vulnerable to fungal infections

5.8 The main functions of the complement system include

A opsonization

B clearance of antibody/antigen complexes

C production of antibodies

D lysis of pathogenic organisms

E production of inflammatory mediators

SECTION 6: CLINICAL ONCOLOGY

6.1 The following cancers progressively increase in incidence from childhood to old age:

    A   carcinoma of the skin
    B   myelomatosis
    C   chronic lymphatic leukaemia
    D   nephroblastoma
    E   Hodgkin's disease

6.2 The following cancers are more common in British women than in British men:

    A   larynx
    B   thyroid
    C   oesophagus
    D   right side of colon
    E   pleural mesothelioma

6.3 The following cancers have a high incidence in the following countries:

    A   stomach cancer in Japan
    B   liver cancer in England
    C   prostatic cancer in the USA
    D   colonic cancer in Nigeria
    E   ovarian cancer in Denmark

6.4 Cancer of the nasopharynx

    A   occurs over three times as commonly in men than in women
    B   has a strong genetic predisposition
    C   is the most common cancer in Southern China
    D   is linked to the Epstein–Barr virus
    E   is more likely to occur in populations over 60 years of age than in younger populations

6.5   The following facts about cancer of the oesophagus are true:

   ✓ A   cancer of the oesophagus is closely related to prolonged smoking and alcohol consumption

  ✗ B   the epidemiological features of cancer of the oesophagus are very similar for Asia and Africa

   ✓ C   there is a high incidence of cancer of the oesophagus in Iran

     D   there has been a very significant fall in the incidence of cancer of the oesophagus in China

     E   cancer of the oesophagus has been linked with zinc deficiency in the soil

6.6   Cancer of the cervix uteri

     A   is rare in Jewesses and Muslim women

     B   is most commonly an adenocarcinoma

     C   occurs more commonly in women who use oral contraceptives

     D   becomes less common in women as their socio-economic status rises

     E   is associated with infection by some types of the human parvovirus

6.7   Bladder cancer is associated with

     A   bladder stones

     B   recurrent urinary tract infections

     C   chronic ingestion of non-steroidal anti-inflammatory medicines

     D   betel eating

     E   obesity

6.8   The following agents have been linked with the following cancers:

     A   phenacetin and leukaemia

     B   azathioprine and non-Hodgkin's lymphoma

     C   combined oral contraceptives and vaginal cancer

     D   melphalan and leukaemia

     E   cyclophosphamide and renal pelvic cancer

6.9 **The following occupations carry an increased risk of the following cancers:**

A radiologists and bone cancer
B farmers and lung cancer
C workers with glues and varnishes and marrow cancer
D seamen and skin cancer
E leather workers and nasal sinus cancer

6.10 **Obesity has been linked with the following cancers:**

A breast
B hepatoma
C gall-bladder
D endometrium
E stomach

6.11 **The following ingredients of food have a protective effect against some cancers:**

A salt
B vitamin
C fibre
D vitamin D
E saturated fat

6.12 **The following viruses are linked with the following human tumours:**

A monkey virus with Burkitt's lymphoma
B papillomavirus with vaginal cancer
C Epstein–Barr virus with laryngeal cancer
D hepatitis B virus with liver cancer
E T-cell leukaemia virus with leukaemia

6.13   The following statements about staging tumours are true:

A   the technique of choice for detecting pulmonary metastases in patients with a normal chest X-ray is CT

B   skeletal X-rays are a sensitive test of the presence of bony metastases and therefore a useful screening test

C   MRI is the only radiographic technique that reliably displays abnormal tissue in marrow

D   the technique of choice for detecting spinal metastases is MRI, with CT a useful alternative

E   ultrasound is the technique of choice for detecting and staging lymphadenopathy of the abdomen and pelvis

6.14   The following cancers are recognized as commonly causing severe hypercalcaemia:

A   stomach cancer

B   thymoma

C   myeloma

D   Hodgkin's disease

E   squamous cell lung cancer

6.15   The principles of combination chemotherapy are

A   to use drugs that are effective when used as single agents in advanced or relapsed disease

B   to use effective single agents in the optimum dose and schedule

C   to combine agents that work through similar biochemical mechanisms to enhance treatment efficacy

D   to combine drugs with similar toxicity to prevent widespread systemic side-effects

E   to combine drugs which have different mechanisms of resistance

6.16 The recognized clinical features of carcinomatous 'meningitis' include

    A   frequent focal fits
    B   ocular muscle palsy
    C   facial weakness
    D   hearing loss
    E   neck stiffness

6.17 Cerebral metastases

    A   will affect about 15% of all cancer patients within their lifetime
    B   are usually extradural
    C   are best diagnosed by computer tomography or magnetic resonance scanning
    D   should be treated with dexamethasone as soon as the diagnosis is made
    E   rarely respond to radiation therapy

6.18 The following statements about the various types of medical radiations are true:

    A   the usual rays used for radiotherapy are X-rays from a linear accelerator
    B   brachytherapy is the delivery of radiotherapy by placing radioactive sources close to the shoulder and lateral chest wall
    C   neutron irradiation is little used nowadays
    D   gamma-rays are useful because there is a relatively sharp reduction of dose beyond a certain tissue depth
    E   electron beams are generated from isotopes such as cobalt-60

6.19 The recognized side-effects of radiotherapy include

    A   indigestion
    B   cystitis
    C   sensory neuropathies
    D   skin pigmentation
    E   cataract

SECTION 7: INFECTION

7.1 **The following organisms are recognized causes of diarrhoea:**

A *Bartonella bacilliformis*
B *Chlamydia trachomatis*
C *Brucella* sp.
D *Pseudomonas aeruginosa*
E *Aeromonas*

7.2 **The following infections are generally milder in children than in adults:**

A schistosomiasis
B poliomyelitis
C mumps
D hepatitis A infection
E yellow fever

7.3 **Fever**

A is due to a resetting of the anterior hypothalamic thermostat at a higher level
B reduces the immune and inflammatory responses to infection
C is linked to the leakage of inflammatory mediators into the blood stream
D is linked to the synthesis of monoamines in the brain
E can occur in the absence of any infective organism

7.4 **The following statements about septic shock are true:**

A the earliest event in septic shock is peripheral vasoconstriction
B capillary walls leak fluid and protein
C a pulmonary toxin appears early on in the course of the condition
D an initial high cardiac output is replaced by an output in the normal range or below
E the serum pH rises

8

7.5 **The following drugs have a bioavailability greater than 80% following oral administration:**

A flucloxacillin
B cephalexin
C ampicillin
D erythromycin
E amoxycillin

7.6 **Patients with a known allergy to penicillin should avoid the following drugs:**

A beta-lactams
B cephalosporins
C monobactams
D carbapenums
E aminoglycosides

7.7 **The following side effects are linked to the following drugs:**

A rigors and amphotericin
B hypoglycaemia and quinine
C beta-lactams and myelosuppression
D ototoxicity and vancomycin
E hypertension and ketoconazole

7.8 **The following statements about travel immunizations are true:**

A diphtheria is the only vaccine for which there is still an international requirement before entry to some countries
B cholera vaccine is no longer recommended by the WHO
C gammaglobulin is derived from pooled blood donations from people with past exposure to hepatitis A
D the active vaccine against hepatitis A is safe, effective and durable
E the standard meningococcal meningitis vaccine is effective in developed countries

7.9   The following statements about travellers' diarrhoea are true:

A   the most common causative agent worldwide is *Giardia lamblia*
B   most infective agents are food and water borne
C   heating water to 50° Centigrade will kill most pathogens
D   water filters are no longer recommended because they frequently
     become colonized by bacteria
E   antimicrobials are rarely indicated

7.10   The following statements about pregnancy and travel are true:

A   commercial airlines will not normally carry a woman who is more
     than 31 weeks pregnant
B   live vaccines should be avoided
C   tetanus immunization is associated with teratogenicity and should
     not be given during pregnancy
D   the only malaria chemoprophylaxis known to be safe during
     pregnancy is chloroquine and proguanil
E   gammaglobulin is safe in pregnancy

7.11   Rhinoviruses may cause

A   gastroenteritis
B   the common cold
C   acute otitis media
D   acute sinusitis
E   pneumonia in children

7.12   Respiratory syncytial virus (RSV)

A   occurs in epidemics and only rarely as sporadic cases
B   affects children primarily when they first go to school
C   is more common in families where the mother smokes
D   has an incubation period of 14–20 days in healthy hosts
E   should be treated with ribavirin in most children

7.13   Influenza vaccines

A   are formalin inactivated
B   contain either two influenza A strains or one B strain
C   are no longer routinely recommended for elderly people unless they
    are at risk, for example they have heart or chest disease
D   are not recommended for normal healthy children
E   are recommended for children with cystic fibrosis

7.14   Ocular herpes

A   may present with fever
B   so rarely causes lymphadenopathy that another diagnosis should be
    considered if lymphadenopathy is found
C   usually causes residual corneal scarring if untreated
D   should be treated with corticosteroids
E   recurs in about one-quarter of patients

7.15   Chickenpox

A   has two reservoirs of infection, humans and monkeys
B   recurs in about 1 in 20 patients
C   is infectious for two days before the rash appears and thereafter
    until the skin lesions are crusted
D   is more likely to lead to zoster if caught during the first year of life
    or by those aged over 65 years
E   may cause encephalitis which has a mortality of over 50%

7.16   Infectious mononucleosis

A   is most conveniently and cheaply diagnosed by the Paul-Bunnell test
B   is more severe in children than adults
C   should be treated with aspirin in adolescents
D   spreads characteristically in epidemics rather than on a sporadic,
    case by case basis
E   is characterized by night sweats and swinging fevers which may
    rise to 40°C

11

7.17 Epstein–Barr virus is linked to (but does not necessarily cause) the following conditions:

✓A   acquired immunodeficiency syndrome (AIDS)
B   Hodgkin's disease
C   toxoplasmosis
D   lymphoma
✗ E   nasopharyngeal carcinoma

7.18 The recognized sequelae of congenital cytomegalovirus include

A   dysphagia
B   dystonia
C   microcephaly
D   chorioretinitis
E   sensorineural hearing loss

7.19 Human orf

A   is a poxvirus disease
B   is usually caught by humans by close person-to-person contact
C   causes a high fever in most cases
D   is diagnosed by electron microscopy
E   should be treated with acyclovir if symptoms warrant it

7.20 Mumps

A   has an incubation period of 5–8 days
B   is transmitted by aerosolized spread, mainly through small droplets
C   may cause a self-limiting lymphocytic meningitis
D   precipitates the development of diabetes in about 5% of cases
E   precipitates abortion in about one-third of affected pregnant women

7.21 MMR vaccine

A   stimulates immunity to measles, mumps and rubella, using dead viruses

B   should be given at 12 months, 5 years and 10 years of age to guarantee lifelong protection

C   has not yet been licensed for usage in the USA

D   is contraindicated in siblings of a child who has had an adverse reaction

E   is now the most common formulation used for childhood measles immunization

7.22 In measles

A   the longer the prodrome the more severe the illness

B   the most common complication to cause death is pneumonia

C   subclinical infection is frequent, occurring in as many as 50% of cases

D   recurrence occurs in about 1 in 10 cases

E   despite immunization worldwide mortality continues to rise

7.23 The following statements about viral food poisoning are true:

A   viruses now account for over three-quarters of all cases of food poisoning

B   several causative viruses can be identified by electron microscopy of vomitus

C   investigation of food poisoning outbreaks must be early because virus excretion is usually transient

D   the only method capable of detecting all known types of virus in a stool is electron microscopy

E   pooled gammaglobulin can give some protection for up to three months following injection

7.24   Rabies virus

A   can penetrate intact mucosa
B   is carried in the saliva of affected animals
C   can be inhaled as an aerosol created by infected bats' nasal
      secretions
D   has never been reported as having been transmitted between
      humans
E   can only replicate in nervous tissue

7.25   The recognized features of rubella include

A   a rash starting on the arms and legs
B   coryza
C   arthralgia of the intervertebral joints
D   mouth ulcers
E   orchitis

7.26   The following statements about rubella vaccination are true:

A   vaccination gives longer lasting immunity than that resulting from
      infection with the wild virus
B   vaccination should be offered to pregnant women who, it is
      suspected, have been exposed to rubella
C   live, attenuated virus is used for the vaccination
D   the most common side-effect in female adult vaccinees are joint
      symptoms
E   vaccinees should be warned that they could pass the infection on to
      susceptible people

Section 7: Infection

7.27 The characteristic features of yellow fever include

A headache
B tachycardia
C iritis
D coated tongue reddened along the edges
E peripheral neuropathy

7.28 The following statements about dengue haemorrhagic fever are correct:

A there is a single vector, the female mosquito *Ae. aegypti*
B in the last 10 years the number of dengue cases worldwide has been dropping
C the condition affects adults more than children
D gross haematuria is rare
E there is no specific drug treatment

7.29 Lassa fever

A mainly occurs in West Africa
B is carried by the rodent *Mastomys natalensis*
C has a mortality of over 50% in affected patients
D causes an acute blindness in about one-half of affected cases
E is effectively treated by ribavirin if given early in the disease

7.30 Ebola virus

A is named after a river in Zaire
B is structurally very similar to Marburg virus
C causes gastrointestinal bleeding
D is highly nephrotoxic
E is effectively treated by ribavirin

15

Section 7: Infection

7.31 In AIDS

A   *P. carinii* is the most common life-threatening opportunistic infection

B   miliary tuberculosis is the most common form of presentation indicating tuberculous infection

C   oropharyngeal candidiasis is the most common and persistent gastrointestinal infection

D   cerebral toxoplasmosis is the most frequent infection of the central nervous system

E   the most common ocular complication is cytomegalovirus retinitis

7.32 The following statements about zidovudine in the management of AIDS are true:

A   there is good clinical evidence that zidovudine reduces the chances of seroconversion following accidental parenteral exposure to HIV-infected blood

B   zidovudine may be useful in reducing the chance of maternal–foetal transmission

C   the huge Anglo-French Concorde trial showed that asymptomatic patients should be treated with zidovudine immediately following seroconversion

D   the most important side-effect of zidovudine is reversible anaemia

E   the incidence of unwanted zidovudine side-effects increases with HIV disease progression

7.33 The following statements about HIV in developing countries are true:

A   HIV-related symptoms appear to start sooner after HIV infection than in developed countries

B   men tend to become infected 5–10 years earlier than women

C   HIV is predominantly transmitted by heterosexual intercourse

D   *Staphylococcus aureus* infection is strongly associated with HIV

E   in many patients the first indication of underlying HIV disease is respiratory tract infection

7.34 **The following statements about diphtheria are true:**

A   people who are Schick negative are likely to develop diphtheria if exposed

B   diphtheria is caused by *Chlamydia diphtheriae*

C   the toxicity of diphtheria toxin depends on the lethal factor A and the spreading factor B

D   diphtheria causes widespread haemorrhage and necrosis of lymphatic tissues which significantly impairs the body's ability to mount an immune response

E   a long-term complication of diphtheria is permanent paralysis of the larynx and pharynx

7.35 ***S. pyogenes* causes the following conditions:**

A   vulvovaginitis

B   perianal disease

C   scarlet fever

D   erysipelas

E   rheumatic fever

7.36 **The following statements about rheumatic fever are true:**

A   infection of the throat is the presenting feature in about one-half of patients with rheumatic fever

B   certain serotypes of the causative organism *S. pyogenes* are more toxic than others

C   a typical attack of rheumatic fever lasts about 6 weeks

D   detection of raised antibody levels or, better, changes in the titre in sequential samples, is often the only reliable evidence of recent infection

E   patients who have had rheumatic carditis are at greater risk of it recurring than those who have not had cardiac complications

7.37   The arthritis of rheumatic fever

A   is migratory
B   affects small joints of hands and feet
C   affects joints symmetrically
D   lasts 2–3 weeks
E   responds to salicylates within 24 hours

7.38   The following statements about the treatment of pneumococcal infections are true:

A   there are substantial areas in the UK and the USA where penicillin-resistant pneumococci are rare
B   in the treatment of meningitis, penicillin has been found to penetrate well into the CSF
C   vancomycin is a cheap alternative to penicillin
D   dexamethasone is now contraindicated in the treatment of pneumococcal meningitis
E   chemoprophylaxis with penicillin should be avoided in children with sickle cell disease

7.39   *S. aureus*

A   produces substances which disrupt red-cell membranes causing haemolysis
B   is linked with toxic shock syndrome
C   is carried permanently in the nose by most people
D   produces beta-lactamase
E   is found to be resistant to erythromycin in over half the patients treated with it

7.40 **The following statements about gonococcus are true:**

A urethral gonorrhoea in men proceeds to epididymo-orchitis in over 50% of cases

B microscopy of suitably stained specimens remains the first diagnostic step despite the recent development of immunological diagnostic reagents

C before the Second World War gonococcus was the most common organism found in bacterial endocarditis

D the cervix is the site most commonly affected in infected women

E treatment of gonococcus with cephalosporins is no longer appropriate in many developing countries because resistance to them has emerged

7.41 **In *Salmonella* infections**

A infection is readily transmitted from person to person

B a *Salmonella*-excreting food handler must usually be suspended from duties

C the incubation period is usually 12–24 hours

D frequent vomiting is the most characteristic symptom

E reactive arthritis is a recognized complication, occurring more commonly in patients with HLA-B27 haplotype

7.42 **In shigellosis**

A the principal route of transmission is person to person

B children may show striking meningism

C the incubation period is 2 to 3 days

D reactive arthritis is common

E the antibiotic of choice, if treatment is needed, is co-trimoxazole

7.43   The following statements about campylobacter enteritis are true:

A   campylobacter enteritis is the most common bacterial infection of the gut in industrialized countries

B   retailed chicken carcasses are almost universally contaminated with campylobacters

C   the infectivity of campylobacters is high because they withstand drying well

D   Guillain-Barré syndrome is a rare but important complication

E   erythromycin is no longer the antibiotic of choice, if treatment is required

7.44   The following organisms which cause food poisoning produce a toxin:

A   *Staphylococcus aureus*

B   *Shigella dysenteriae*

C   *Bacillus cereus*

D   *Clostridium botulinum*

E   *Vibrio parahaemolyticus*

7.45   The recognized clinical features of typhoid include

A   a fever which rises slowly and then plateaus, showing little diurnal variation

B   headache

C   diarrhoea early in the course of the disease followed by constipation

D   temperature–pulse dissociation

E   hypertension

7.46   Cholera

A   does not significantly affect any other species but man

B   starts with very painful colic and diarrhoea

C   affects children less severely than adults

D   responds dramatically in most cases to tetracycline

E   can be effectively prevented in endemic areas by immunization

7.47   The following statements about whooping cough are true:

A   whooping cough is caused by *Bordetella pertussis*, a small, anaerobic organism with characteristics of both viruses and bacteria

B   fever is unusual in whooping cough so its presence suggests a secondary bacterial infection

C   bronchiectasis is a common complication of whooping cough

D   passive immunization with immunoglobin is indicated in acute, severe cases

E   pertussis vaccines are not usually given after the age of 6 because of local reactions

7.48   Plague

A   is caused by *Yersinia pestis*, a small non-sporing bacillus

B   is transmitted among animals by fleas and by ingestion of contaminated animal tissues

C   is characterized by the appearance of painless buboes

D   has been called 'Black Death' because of the appearance of purpuric lesions which may become necrotic, leading to gangrene of distal extremities

E   should be treated, as the antibiotic of first choice, by high dose penicillin

7.49   Yersiniosis

A   is caused by two bacteria, *Yersinia enterocolitica* and *Yersinia pseudotuberculosis*

B   is a disease of developed, industrialized countries

C   may mimic acute appendicitis in its presentation

D   may present with extraintestinal signs including pharyngitis and cellulitis

E   should be treated with tetracycline as soon as the diagnosis is made

7.50   The following statements about brucellosis are true:

A   the worldwide incidence of brucellosis is falling

B   in endemic areas, hand to hand contact is the most common form
     of transmission

C   brucellosis may be transmitted sexually or by blood transfusion

D   brucellosis is rare in children

E   brucellosis may be complicated by arthritis followed by spondylitis

7.51   Tetanus

A   achieves its clinical effect by producing a toxin which paralyses
     muscles by blocking calcium uptake

B   is caused by a Gram-positive bacillus which will only grow in
     anaerobic conditions

C   occurs more commonly after minor wounds than major wounds

D   has an incubation period which can range from 1 day to 2 months

E   confers life-long immunity for those patients who recover

7.52   The treatment of severe tetanus involves the following measures:

A   all patients requiring hospital admission should be given equine
     antiserum or human immunoglobulin

B   intrathecal tetanus antiserum is indicated for patients with spinal
     paralysis

C   local infiltration of tetanus antitoxin is indicated for the wound
     once it has been treated according to surgical principles

D   tracheostomy is indicated for moderate (Grade II) tetanus

E   penicillin is routinely given

7.53   The following statements about tuberculosis are true:

A   adverse reactions to BCG vaccination are rare and often due to faulty technique

B   the overall mortality from tuberculosis in developed countries is now less than 1%

C   following diagnosis, most patients with tuberculosis need hospitalization for purposes of isolation and stabilization on therapy

D   10% of close contacts of patients with sputum smear-positive tuberculosis will develop the disease

E   at least 30% of those with concurrent HIV and *M. tuberculosis* infections will develop overt tuberculosis

7.54   The following radiological features are characteristic of post-primary pulmonary tuberculosis:

A   mediastinal enlargement

B   right ventricular hypertrophy

C   small (less than 1 cm diameter) nodules throughout the lung fields

D   calcification

E   unilateral or bilateral nodular shadowing in the upper lobes

7.55   Leprosy

A   is reliably diagnosed by the Heaf test

B   can be passed by untreated lactating mothers to their babies through breast milk

C   is most successfully treated with multi-drug therapy

D   affects peripheral nerves such as the ulnar, median and great auricular

E   remains localized in distribution provided the patient only develops a low degree of cell-mediated immunity

7.56   The recognized complications of Lyme disease include

A   arthritis
B   atrioventricular block
C   meningoencephalitis
D   cardiomegaly
E   conjunctivitis

7.57   The characteristic features of leptospirosis include

A   intense, throbbing frontal headache
B   splenomegaly
C   erythema nodosum
D   myalgia
E   temporary deafness in one or both ears

7.58   The following statements about treponemal infections are true:

A   a patient with venereal syphilis has immunity against yaws
B   yaws is caused by *Treponema pallidum*
C   venereal syphilis can be acquired by children by non-sexual, social contact with adults with the disease
D   bejel is the only type of endemic syphilis still prevalent
E   the lesion of yaws and other treponematoses is largely due to the host's immune response to the treponeme

7.59   Recognized complications of Legionnaire's disease include

A   hepatitis
B   acute respiratory failure
C   acute renal failure
D   splenomegaly
E   osteomyelitis

7.60 Cat scratch disease

A   is not always caused by the scratch of a cat
B   causes regional lymphadenopathy
C   is diagnosed by a positive Frei skin test
D   is effectively treated by penicillin
E   is caused by *Rochalimaea henselae* in most cases

7.61 Chlamydiae have a significant role in the aetiology of the following conditions:

A   acute symptomatic prostatitis
B   bartholinitis
C   bacterial vaginosis
D   vaginitis
E   epididymo-orchitis

7.62 Psittacosis

A   mostly affects children
B   varies in presentation from a mild influenza-like illness to a fulminating toxic illness with multiple organ involvement
C   rarely causes extrapulmonary complications
D   can cause abortion
E   is best diagnosed, for the purposes of litigation, by a combination of microscopy and serology

7.63 Systemic fungal infections occur in the following:

A   mycetoma
B   pityriasis versicolor
C   histoplasmosis
D   blastomycosis
E   paracoccidioidomycosis

7.64 **The following drugs have a useful role in the treatment of amoebiasis:**

    A   tinidazole
    B   chloroquine
    C   metronidazole
    D   proguanil
    E   erythromycin

7.65 **The female *Anopheles* mosquito**

    A   needs a blood meal before egg laying
    B   prefers to bite humans in the early morning
    C   exists in the UK and is capable of transmitting imported malaria strains
    D   lays her eggs at many, indiscriminately selected breeding sites which makes control difficult
    E   can be distinguished from other mosquitoes by the angle at which the adult inclines her body while feeding

7.66 **In cerebral malaria**

    A   patients commonly present with neck rigidity indicating meningism
    B   mechanical obstruction to the brain's micro-circulation is now thought to be the main mechanism leading to coma
    C   papilloedema is very rare
    D   patients who survive very rarely suffer long-term sequelae
    E   treatment with dexamethasone reduces length of coma

SECTION 8: CHEMICAL AND PHYSICAL INJURIES AND CLIMATIC AND OCCUPATIONAL DISEASES

8.1   Antidotes of proven value exist for poisoning by

A   opiate analgesics
B   paracetamol
C   benzodiazepines
D   aspirin
E   barbiturates

8.2   Gastric lavage for self-poisoning

A   may increase the severity of poisoning by flushing drug from the stomach into the small bowel, thus facilitating rapid absorption
B   is indicated in severe cases of poisoning up to 4 hours after ingestion of the poison
C   deters the recipient from further episodes of self-poisoning
D   is contraindicated in patients who have ingested petroleum distillates
E   is contraindicated in unconscious patients

8.3   Tricyclic antidepressant overdosage

A   alone or in conjunction with other drugs causes, on average, one death a day in England and Wales
B   may cause a rapid rise in blood pressure
C   causes death in most patients if more than 250 mg has been ingested
D   may require charcoal haemoperfusion if the patient is comatose
E   causes most of its clinically important effects within 6 hours of ingestion

8.4 **The recognized features of an episode of severe ethanol intoxication (blood levels greater than 3000 mg/l) include**

   A   double vision
   B   hypothermia
   C   hyperreflexia
   D   hypoglycaemia
   E   convulsions

8.5 **The following industrial processes are linked with the following cancers:**

   A   furniture manufacturing and cancer of the nasal sinus
   B   working in the rubber industry and bladder cancer
   C   working as a painter and skin cancer
   D   boot and shoe manufacture and lip cancer
   E   iron and steel founding and lung cancer

8.6 **Repetitive strain injury is recognized to affect**

   A   musicians
   B   coal-face workers
   C   dancers
   D   hairdressers
   E   machine operators

8.7 **The following statements about acute mountain sickness are true:**

   A   females are more prone than males
   B   young children are prone to pulmonary oedema
   C   acute mountain sickness is more common in those who have in the past suffered badly from the condition
   D   fast ascents of mountains are less likely to cause acute mountain sickness
   E   independent of speed of ascent, severe exertion predisposes to acute mountain sickness

SECTION 9: PRINCIPLES OF CLINICAL PHARMACOLOGY AND DRUG THERAPY

9.1   **The following statements about the therapeutic index of a drug are true:**

A   the therapeutic index of drugs is a scale between 1 and 100 in which drugs with many benefits have a high number and those with many side-effects have a low number

B   penicillin has a high therapeutic index

C   aminoglycoside antibiotics have a low therapeutic index

D   the risk:benefit ratio for a particular drug will be more favourable if it has a high therapeutic index

E   if there is a choice between two drugs, each of which has equal efficacy, one would choose the one with the higher therapeutic index

9.2   **The following statements about the oral absorption of drugs are true:**

A   first-pass metabolism is defined as the metabolism in the liver that occurs before the drug enters the systemic circulation

B   the absorption of some drugs is increased in patients with coeliac disease

C   in migraine the rate of drug absorption is reduced

D   enteric-coated formulations are better absorbed than drugs without enteric coating when there is severe diarrhoea

E   drinking milk impairs tetracycline absorption

9.3   **The following drugs are more likely than most to cause anaphylactic shock**

A   penicillin

B   rifampicin

C   streptomycin

D   local anaesthetics

E   glyceryl trinitrate

SECTION 10: NUTRITION

10.1 **The recognized features of kwashiorkor include**

A age between 5–10 years
B fine, friable discoloured hair
C significant loss of muscle mass
D hepatomegaly
E skin rash

10.2 **The following changes in hormonal balance occur in malnutrition:**

A low growth hormone levels
B low insulin levels
C low catecholamine levels
D low cortisol levels
E high free and bound thyroxine levels

10.3 **In malnutrition**

A the stomach produces more acid than usual causing an increase in peptic ulceration
B the pancreas is atrophied and fewer digestive enzymes than normal are produced
C there is loss of intestinal motility
D there is increased gastrointestinal absorption of any food eaten
E there is small intestinal atrophy with reduced levels of digestive enzymes

10.4 **The recognized features of anorexia nervosa include**

A low birth weight, 15% or more below the expected weight of the person
B male sex in as many as 25% of cases
C self-induced vomiting
D a loss of axillary and pubic hair
E early morning waking

10.5   In the treatment of bulimia nervosa

A   initial hospitalization is required for most patients
B   cognitive behaviour therapy is the most effective treatment
    available
C   antidepressants have a role as second line therapy
D   appetite suppressants have a role as second line therapy
E   more than half the patients go on to develop other psychiatric conditions

10.6   The following statements about obesity are true:

A   with increasing age the distribution of fat alters towards a greater
    proportion subcutaneously rather than intraperitoneally
B   in surveys the prevalence of obesity among men declines after the
    age of 50
C   in surveys the prevalence of obesity among women in developed
    countries is greater than among men
D   obese people are very insulin sensitive which makes them prone to
    diabetes
E   in developed countries there is an inverse relationship between
    obesity and socio-economic class

**10.7   Obese people are more prone than lean people to the following
       conditions:**

A   polycystic disease
B   infertility in men
C   stomach cancer
D   pancreatitis
E   prostate cancer

10.8 **The following statements about minerals and trace elements are true:**

A   patients on intravenous nutrition should have their intravenous intake of trace elements matched to their normal oral intake

B   significant gastrointestinal fluid losses affect sodium homoeostasis less than potassium homoeostasis

C   potassium requirements may double in patients receiving amphotericin B

D   patients with significant gastrointestinal losses may have substantially greater requirements for zinc

E   sodium restriction may be necessary in patients with chronic hepatic failure

10.9 **Recognized complications of enteral feeding in hospital include**

A   nausea and vomiting

B   disturbances in plasma potassium

C   diarrhoea

D   constipation

E   bloating

10.10 **Coca-Cola® has the following useful functions:**

A   stimulating intellectual activity in patients with cerebral palsy

B   unblocking enteral nutrition tubes

C   stimulating lactation in mothers experiencing difficulties breast feeding

D   rehydrating dehydrated children, particularly those with diarrhoea

E   destroying viral warts on hands and feet if these extremities are bathed daily in Coca-Cola®

SECTION 11: METABOLIC DISORDERS

11.1 **The following procedures are used in pre-natal diagnosis of inborn errors of metabolism:**

A   analysis of cultured amniotic cells obtained by amniocentesis before the 10th week of pregnancy

B   direct examination of the foetus by ultrasonography

C   direct examination of the foetus by fetoscopy

D   DNA examination of a single cell removed at the eight-cell stage of an embryo produced by *in vitro* fertilization

E   DNA analysis of chorionic villi obtained by biopsy at the eighth to tenth week of pregnancy

11.2 **The following diseases are classified as glycogen storage diseases:**

A   Ehlers-Danlos syndrome

B   Niemann-Pick disease

C   McArdle's disease

D   Pompe's disease

E   von Gierke's disease

11.3 **The following risk factors predispose to gout:**

A   smoking

B   alcohol consumption

C   the use of ACE inhibitor drugs

D   the use of diuretics

E   occupational environmental lead exposure

33

11.4 The following statements about gout are true:

A   gout is seldom seen in women before the menopause
B   the renal insufficiency linked to gout does not reduce life
    expectancy in most cases
C   hypertension occurs in up to one-half of patients with gout
D   hypertriglyceridaemia occurs in more than three-quarters of
    patients with gout
E   the tophi found in gout contain large amounts of cheesy lipid
    material

**11.5 The following disorders are transmitted as an autosomal dominant
trait:**

A   familial juvenile gouty nephropathy
B   galactosaemia
C   Fanconi syndrome
D   cystinosis
E   phenylketonuria

11.6 The following factors may precipitate acute porphyria:

A   unaccustomed exercise
B   fasting
C   a diet rich in phenylalanine
D   intercurrent infection
E   food with a high amine content

11.7 **The following drugs are unsafe for use in patients with acute porphyria:**

A   enalapril
B   flucloxacillin
C   gentamicin
D   temazepam
E   metoclopramide

11.8 **Heterozygous familial hypercholesterolaemia**

A   is the most common genetic disorder in Britain and the USA
B   does not express itself as raised serum cholesterol levels until adulthood
C   is characterized by the presence of tendon xanthomata
D   causes most affected patients to be overweight
E   causes decreased catabolism of low density lipoprotein

11.9 **The following statements about the treatment of hyperlipidaemia are true:**

A   patients whose serum total cholesterol persists above 8 mmol/l, despite a lipid-lowering diet, need lipid-lowering drug therapy even if no other risk factors for heart disease exist
B   lipid-lowering drug therapy is indicated for patients with proven coronary heart disease should their serum cholesterol persist above about 6.5 mmol/l despite an appropriate diet
C   an appropriate diet usually has a dramatic effect in lowering serum cholesterol levels in patients with familial hypercholesterolaemia
D   hormone replacement therapy often decreases serum low density lipoprotein cholesterol and raises serum high density lipoprotein cholesterol thus providing an alternative therapy for peri- or post-menopausal women
E   lipid-lowering drugs may reduce femoral and carotid atheroma

11.10 Copper

    A   homoeostasis depends on its excretion in bile
    B   is transported loosely bound to albumin
    C   deficiency results in Wilson's disease
    D   overload results in Menke's disease
    E   is essential for neuromuscular conduction

11.11 The recognized features of zinc deficiency include

    A   mental retardation
    B   increased susceptibility to infection
    C   hirsutism
    D   bullous dermatitis
    E   constipation

11.12 The recognized features of Type I Gaucher's disease include

    A   pathological fractures
    B   burning paraesthesiae in the extremities
    C   grey-brown pigmentation of the forehead, hands and pretibial region
    D   anaemia
    E   progressive motor weakness

11.13 Diabetes mellitus may occur as a secondary consequence of the following conditions:

    A   chronic pancreatitis
    B   albinism
    C   acromegaly
    D   Addison's disease
    E   haemochromatosis

11.14 Foot ulcers are more common in diabetic patients as a consequence of

    A   loss of collagen causing reduced thickness and elasticity of the skin
    B   venous congestion
    C   poor lymphatic drainage
    D   diseased small blood vessels
    E   motor neuropathy

11.15 The following statements are correct within the framework of the modern classification of diabetes mellitus:

    A   type I diabetes appears to result from destruction of the Islets of Langerhans caused by multiple small calculi in the fine branches of the pancreatic duct
    B   type I diabetes typically occurs before the age of 30 but can occur at any age
    C   most type I diabetic patients can be managed on a combination of diet and oral hypoglycaemic drugs
    D   type II diabetes is characterized by the presence of circulating islet cell antibodies
    E   type III diabetes appears confined to those born in the tropics

11.16 The secretion of insulin is stimulated by

    A   sympathetic nerve stimulation
    B   glucagon
    C   dopamine
    D   somatostatin
    E   acetylcholine

11.17 Dietary treatment of diabetes mellitus should be guided by the following principles:

A small, frequent meals are more suitable than one or two large ones
B foods with a high fibre content should be avoided because they slow carbohydrate metabolism
C the carbohydrate content of the diet should provide about half of the total calorie intake
D fat should not contribute more than 35% of total calorie intake
E mono-unsaturated fatty acids should be excluded from the diet as far as possible

11.18 The following statements about sulphonylureas are true:

A sulphonylureas act by stimulating intracellular phosphorylation
B the hypoglycaemic effectiveness usually stays constant over many years in most patients
C some sulphonylureas can cause bone marrow depression
D sulphonylureas are particularly effective in young, thin type I diabetic patients
E sulphonylureas should not be combined with biguanides

11.19 Human insulin

A is closer to porcine than bovine insulin in molecular structure
B is markedly less antigenic than either bovine or porcine insulin
C is believed to be more rapidly absorbed from the injection site than porcine insulin
D is particularly liable to cause fat atrophy at injection sites
E is about 2.5 times more effective, on an equimolar basis, than porcine insulin

11.20 The rate of absorption of insulin after subcutaneous injection can be speeded by:

A   deep rather than shallow subcutaneous injection
B   massage
C   hot baths
D   resting quietly
E   the use of the abdomen rather than the thigh or arm

11.21 The following statements about the prognosis of diabetes mellitus are true:

A   there has been an improvement in the morbidity, but not the mortality, of diabetic patients in the last 20 years
B   a type I diabetic patient diagnosed before the age of 10 has a less than 10% chance of achieving the age of 50
C   foot ulceration is a complication predominantly of type II diabetics
D   stroke is the second most common cause of death, after cardiac causes, in diabetic patients
E   visual complications in type II diabetics are more likely to be cataract   than proliferative retinopathy

11.22 The following statements about diabetic retinopathy are true:

A   the fasting blood glucose may need to be consistently below 7 mmol/l and the post-prandial blood glucose below 9 mmol/l if the risk of retinopathy is to be reduced substantially
B   diabetic patients should have an eye examination annually
C   over 50% of patients will have ophthalmoscopic evidence of retinopathy at diagnosis
D   ophthalmoscopic evidence of retinopathy occurs in most diabetic patients within 20 years of diagnosis
E   proliferative change is more likely in younger patients

11.23 Recognized features of amyloidosis include

A thyroid enlargement
B cardiomyopathy
C uveitis
D dermatomyositis
E macroglossia

11.24 The anion gap is increased in

A diabetic ketoacidosis
B classical renal tubular acidosis
C salicylate-induced acidosis
D lactic acidosis
E uraemic acidosis

SECTION 12: ENDOCRINE DISORDERS

12.1   Adrenocorticotrophin (ACTH)

  A   stimulates the pituitary to secrete cortisol
  B   is regulated by hypothalamic corticotrophin releasing hormone and vasopressin
  C   plasma concentrations are low in the evening
  D   plasma concentrations are low in Addison's disease
  E   plasma concentrations are low in Nelson's syndrome

12.2   Growth hormone deficiency

  A   is best diagnosed by a random serum growth hormone estimation
  B   in the mother reduces growth of the foetus *in utero*
  C   in children is usually accompanied by delayed puberty
  D   occurs in anorexia nervosa
  E   occurs in type I diabetes mellitus

12.3   The indications for pituitary tumour surgery include

  A   sudden visual compromise
  B   Cushing's disease not cured by pituitary radiation in children
  C   an expanding prolactinoma even if plasma prolactin levels are normal
  D   a tumour extending into both cavernous sinuses
  E   a prolactinoma extending above the pituitary fossa which is unresponsive to treatment with bromocriptine or other dopamine agonists

12.4   The recognized features of acromegaly include

  A   acne
  B   marked spinal stiffness
  C   galactorrhoea in women
  D   obstructive sleep apnoea
  E   mitral stenosis

12.5 The following statements about thyroid function are true:

A   the thyroid stores minimal amounts of hormone

B   thyroglobulin is the main protein in the plasma which binds thyroid hormones

C   most T4 is derived from enzymatic conversion of T3 in the plasma, with a small fraction being secreted directly by the thyroid

D   TSH is secreted by the anterior pituitary, its main function being to regulate thyroid hormones

E   the cellular site of action for thyroid hormones is the nucleus

12.6 The recognized features of Cushing's syndrome include

F   A   growth spurt in children

F ⌐ T   B   distal myopathy

F   C   proximal sensory neuropathy

T   D   loss of scalp hair

T   E   bruising

12.7 In the investigation of Cushing's syndrome

F A   the measurement of free levels of plasma cortisol is the mostly commonly performed definitive test

f   B   the measurement of random morning cortisol levels is a useful diagnostic test

C   plasma ACTH assay is valuable in defining an adrenal cause

T   D   the dexamethasone suppression test has high sensitivity in the diagnosis of Cushing's syndrome

f   E   hyperkalaemia is a frequent finding

SECTION 13: PREGNANCY

13.1   The benefits of combined oral contraceptives include

A   suppression of menorrhagia
B   lessened risk of benign breast disease
C   lessened risk of cancer of the ovary
D   lessened risk of cancer of the breast
E   lessened risk of cancer of the cervix

13.2   The following oral antihypertensive agents may safely be used throughout pregnancy:

⊤ A   methyldopa
B   beta-blockers
C   ACE inhibitors
D   prazosin
E   clonidine

13.3   The following physiological changes occur during normal pregnancy:

A   peripheral vasodilation
B   a fall in stroke volume
C   a fall in tidal lung volume
D   a soft diastolic murmur
E   a fall in red cell mass resulting in anaemia

SECTION 14: GASTROENTEROLOGY

14.1   Vomiting which occurs

A   in the morning is associated with uraemia
B   during meals is linked to psychological disorders
C   immediately after meals is associated with gall bladder disease
D   an hour or more after meals is associated with gastric carcinoma
E   in a projectile fashion may result from raised intracranial pressure

14.2   Pain from

A   intestinal distension may be referred into the leg
B   the colon is often poorly localized
C   the stomach is transmitted via the vagus nerve
D   the pancreas is relieved by lying flat
E   the small intestine is felt in the midline

14.3   Recognized causes of constipation include

A   Crohn's disease
B   hyperthyroidism
C   hypocalcaemia
D   Parkinson's disease
E   pudendal nerve damage

14.4   The following statements about the management of acute gastrointestinal bleeding are true:

A   central venous pressure lines should be avoided in patients over 65 because of the known high rate of complications
B   transfusion should aim to raise the haemoglobin to at least 10 g/dl in most patients
C   in general 1 unit of blood raises the haemoglobin by 2 g/dl in an adult
D   the insertion of a nasogastric tube is indicated in most patients, primarily to check for rebleeding
E   the routine use of H_2-antagonists is indicated in most patients to reduce gastric acid secretion

14.5   Dental caries

A   is more prevalent in elderly people than in young adults
B   is promoted more effectively by glucose than by sucrose
C   does not occur unless the pH at the enamel surface falls below about 5.5
D   destroys dentine more quickly than enamel
E   can be prevented if adults and children use toothpaste containing fluoride

14.6   Recurrent oral ulcers

A   affect up to one-third of Western populations
B   are linked to vitamin deficiencies
C   appear to affect some families more than others
D   affect people aged over 50 more than younger populations
E   may extend to involve vulvovaginal sites as part of Reiter's disease

14.7   Recognized causes of xerostomia (dry mouth) include

A   chemotherapy
B   hepatitis
C   hypertensive drugs
D   diabetes
E   anaemia

14. 8   The following statements about the treatment of oesophageal reflux are true:

A   stopping smoking will usually result in a very significant improvement in reflux

B   avoidance of large meals is no longer recommended for treating reflux

C   proton-pump inhibitors are more useful than H_2-receptor antagonists because of their effectiveness in reducing acid secretion, particularly when food stimulated

D   long term acid suppression maintains patients symptom free, but withdrawal is usually associated with relapse

E   there are concerns about the safety of long-term acid suppression in the treatment of reflux because of good evidence linking this form of treatment to oesophageal carcinoma

14.9   Achalasia

A   is best investigated and diagnosed by barium swallow

B   is characterized by painless dysphagia

C   causes swallowing difficulties with fluids rather than solids

D   can cause respiratory symptoms

E   is now effectively treated with drugs such as calcium antagonists rather than, as previously, oesophagomyotomy

14.10   The following drugs are recognized causes of oesophageal injury:

A   folic acid supplements

B   tetracycline

C   captopril

D   slow-release theophylline

E   erythromycin

14.11 The following facts about duodenal ulceration are true:

A   virtually all patients with duodenal ulcers are colonized by
    H. pylori

B   eradication of *H. pylori* leads to the healing of duodenal ulcers but
    has no effect on the incidence of ulcer relapse

C   duodenal ulcers do not occur in anacidic patients

D   patients with duodenal ulcer secrete no more acid, on average, than
    healthy people

E   patients with duodenal ulcer occur more commonly in urban rather
    than rural populations

14.12 In the Zollinger–Ellison syndrome

A   the fasting plasma gastrin is raised

B   there is usually a pancreatic tumour easily found at laparotomy

C   injection of secretin as part of the secretin test causes a fall in
    plasma gastrin

D   the H_2 antagonists are the medication of choice

E   diarrhoea occurs in over one-third of patients

14.13 Gastrin

A   is released in response to protein ingestion

B   is secreted in response to the presence of *H. pylori* in the stomach

C   stimulates gastric pepsin secretion as its main action

D   is mainly found in the gastric antrum

E   is released in excessive amounts in patients with duodenal ulcer

14.14 The recognized features of the carcinoid syndrome include

A   polyuria

B   amenorrhoea

C   cardiac valve abnormalities

D   secretory diarrhoea

E   flushing

14.15 Coeliac disease

A   affects the small and large intestine
B   is characterized by loss of villous height
C   is characterized by significant loss of intestinal mucosal thickness
D   is best diagnosed by a barium meal and follow-through
E   may be complicated by a T-cell lymphoma

14.16 The recognized features of Whipple's disease include

A   vitiligo
B   finger clubbing
C   arthritis
D   pleurisy
E   hypertension

14.17 Tropical sprue

A   occurs predominantly in Africa
B   occurs mostly in children
C   rarely presents with diarrhoea
D   is caused by an *E. coli* enterotoxin
E   shows histological changes in both small and large bowel

14.18 Crohn's disease

A   particularly affects people from the higher social classes
B   is negatively associated with smoking
C   occurs more commonly in both partners of marriages, suggesting
     there is an environmental factor in the aetiology of the disease
D   commonly affects the whole of the gastrointestinal tract
     histologically, although this involvement may only be apparent
     clinically in segments
E   is complicated by amyloid, which can occur both within the bowel
     and systemically

14.19 **In a young adult presenting with diarrhoea and malaise the following features would suggest Crohn's disease rather than ulcerative colitis:**

A   an abdominal mass
B   bloody diarrhoea
C   pneumaturia
D   marked inflammation of the rectum on sigmoidoscopy
E   the presence of fleshy anal skin tags

14.20 **Ulcerative colitis**

A   occurs almost exclusively in Western populations
B   is becoming more common
C   usually presents with a gradual onset of symptoms
D   is best kept in remission by a small dose of corticosteroids
E   does not reduce the fertility of affected women

14.21 **The following statement about gastrointestinal motility are true:**

A   the gastrointestinal tract is composed of two muscle layers, one circular and one longitudinal
B   denervated small bowel smooth muscle exhibits continuous contractile activity implying that, in man, neural activity is predominantly inhibitory
C   the parasympathetic nervous supply to the gut as far as the proximal gut is supplied by the vagus, the fibres of which are mostly sensory
D   the average transit time through the small bowel is 3 hours
E   during sleep the colon is particularly active which explains why many people wish to open their bowels in the early morning

14.22 Following gastrointestinal surgery

A   ileus occurs as a consequence of neural rather than muscular dysfunction

B   motor activity returns within a few hours to the stomach

C   recovery from ileus can be hastened by defunctioning the small bowel by naso-gastric aspiration

D   bile acids will damage the gastric mucosa if the pyloric sphincter is damaged and unable to prevent the reflux of duodenal contents into the antrum

E   non-obstructive gastric stasis is an expected long-term sequel of vagotomy

14.23 Characteristic findings in the irritable bowel syndrome include

A   inflammation of the rectal and sigmoid mucosa

B   thickened colon on palpation

C   diagnostic appearances on barium enema

D   normal blood sedimentation rate

E   absence of blood in the faeces

14.24 The following statements about colonic diverticular disease are true:

A   high basal intracolonic pressure is characteristic

B   diverticula usually occur at the site where colonic blood vessels penetrate the wall

C   diabetic patients are prone to diverticular disease

D   a fully developed diverticulum is covered by mucosa, connective tissue and peritoneum but no muscle

E   there is rarely any narrowing of the colonic lumen

14.25 Recognized presenting features of oesophageal carcinoma include

A finger clubbing
B hoarseness
C cervical lymph nodes
D intermittent dysphagia
E Bell's palsy

14.26 The following statements about gastric carcinoma are true

A there is a low incidence in the USA
B early reports linking *H. pylori* to gastric carcinoma have now been disproved
C patients with proven benign gastric ulcers have an increased risk of subsequently developing gastric cancer
D mass screening in Japan has proved a cost effective measure
E the antrum of the stomach is the area most commonly affected

14.27 The following statements about small bowel tumours are true:

A less than 5% of all malignant gastrointestinal tumours occur in the small bowel
B the small bowel is the most common site in the gastrointestinal tract for metastatic melanomas
C carcinoid tumour is the most common small bowel malignancy
D over 90% of patients with familial adenomatosis polyposis of the small gut develop a carcinoma
E coeliac disease is associated with an increased incidence of adenocarcinoma of the small bowel.

14.28 **The following statements about Duke's classification of colorectal tumours are true:**

A a Duke's A tumour affects the mucosa but has not penetrated the muscularis mucosa

B a Duke's B tumour has penetrated the bowel wall but not extended to lymph nodes

C a Duke's C tumour has metastasised to lymph nodes

D a patient with a Duke's A tumour has a 95–100% chance of surviving five years following prompt resection

E a patient with a Duke's C tumour has a less than 5% chance of surviving five years following prompt resection

14.29 **Chronic intestinal ischaemia**

A is usually due to atheroma of the inferior mesenteric artery

B classically causes cramping abdominal pain 1–2 hours after eating a meal

C can be diagnosed angiographically with the proviso that the extent of the stenotic lesion is not related to the severity of symptoms

D can be diagnosed accurately by the finding of a loud systolic bruit on auscultation of the abdomen

E is successfully treated by vascular surgery in a high percentage of cases

14.30 **Non-infective causes of diarrhoea include**

A zinc poisoning

B mushroom poisoning

C poisoning with poorly refrigerated fish

D medullary carcinoma of the thyroid

E non-beta islet-cell tumours

14.31 The following inherited metabolic disorders affecting the liver cause the following features:

A   primary haemochromatosis causes haemolytic anaemia
B   alpha$_1$-antitrypsin deficiency causes emphysema
C   porphyria cutanea tardia causes pigmentation
D   primary biliary cirrhosis causes pruritus
E   Wilson's disease causes skin light sensitivity and behavioural disorders

14.32 Recognized causes of acute pancreatitis include

A   hepatitis
B   peptic ulcers
C   erythromycin
D   Coxsackie B virus
E   corticosteroids

14.33 The features of severe acute pancreatitis include

A   vomiting, particularly in the first 12 hours
B   epigastric pain which gets progressively worse over the first 72 hours
C   paralytic ileus
D   absence of fever
E   pleural effusion

14.34 The complications of chronic pancreatitis include

A   hyperparathyroidism
B   splenic vein thrombosis
C   diabetes
D   non-diabetic retinopathy
E   chronic glossitis

14.35 Recognized presentations of carcinoma of the pancreas include

  A   diabetes mellitus
  B   thrombophlebitis
  C   bleeding from oesophageal varices
  D   icterus
? E   bone pain

14.36 In acute cholecystitis

  A   there is an association with gallstones in about a third of cases
  B   the right hypochondrial pain usually subsides within about 18 hours
  C   serum bilirubin concentrations can rise in uncomplicated cases without there necessarily being a stone in the bile duct
  D   ultrasound is the preferred radiological investigation
  E   antibiotics are indicated only in patients with a fever

14.37 A haemolytic cause for jaundice is suggested by the following findings:

  A   bilirubinuria
  B   reticulocytosis
  C   anaemia
  D   raised serum transaminase levels
  E   splenomegaly

14.38 In hepatitis A virus infection

  A   the incubation period is between 15–50 days
  B   the most common form of transmission is hand to hand contact
  C   patients aged under 30 are usually anicteric throughout the course of the illness
  D   the diagnosis is usually made under electron microscopy by visualizing the virus in the patient's blood
  E   bedrest does not accelerate recovery

SECTION 15: CARDIOLOGY

15.1   In the cardiac action potential

A   phase 0 represents the phase of rapid efflux of Na^+ ions
B   phase 0 represents the phase of rapid efflux of K^+ ions
C   phase 1 represents the phase of efflux of K^+ ions
D   phase 2 represents the phase of Ca^{++} influx
E   phase 3 is recognized as the phase of repolarization

15.2   In the normal cardiac cycle

A   atrial contraction contributes about a third of total ventricular
    filling
B   aortic and pulmonary valve closure is coincident with a rise in
    ventricular pressure
C   90% of end-diastolic ventricular volume is ejected during systole
D   aortic closure precedes pulmonary closure
E   a fourth heart sound can be a normal finding in young people

15.3   In the normal heart

A   the 'a' wave in the right atrium is less than 7 mmHg
B   normal mean pulmonary artery pressure is less than 35 mmHg
C   normal left ventricular end-diastolic pressure is less than 25 mmHg
D   the left ventricular end-diastolic pressure equals left atrial pressure
    at the end of diastole
E   pulmonary vascular resistance equals the difference between the
    mean aortic and right atrial pressure divided by the cardiac output

15.4   Chest pain

A   in aortic stenosis is most probably caused by the presence of
    unsuspected coronary artery disease
B   occurring in mitral stenosis can be caused by myocardial ischaemia
C   related to myocardial infarction occurs most commonly in the evening
D   related to oesophageal pathology is not helped by anti-anginal
    therapy
E   due to Tietze's syndrome carries a poor prognosis

15.5 **The following conditions are recognized cardiovascular causes of syncope:**

A   aortic dissection
B   mitral regurgitation
C   pulmonary hypertension
D   left atrial myxoma
E   pericarditis

15.6 **On a chest X-ray**

A   the right border of the cardiac silhouette is formed by the right ventricle
B   the left atrium is posterior on a lateral projection
C   enlargement of central and peripheral pulmonary arteries is seen in pulmonary hypertension
D   pulmonary oligaemia is typical of Fallot's tetralogy
E   calcification of the coronary arteries implies significant coronary artery stenosis

15.7 **The following statements are true of the electrocardiogram:**

A   an inverted T wave in V1 is a normal finding
B   the maximum QRS duration must not exceed 140 msec
C   a dominant R wave in V1 is normal in children
D   T wave inversion is always abnormal if present in leads V4 to V6
E   the normal frontal axis is between $+30°$ and $-90°$

15.8 **The following are causes of a false positive exercise test response:**

A   hyperventilation
B   Wolff-Parkinson-White syndrome
C   mitral valve prolapse
D   lithium therapy
E   hypertrophic cardiomyopathy

15.9   In heart failure

A   milrinone increases ejection fraction
B   milrinone improves prognosis
C   a poor prognosis is indicated by hyponatraemia
D   non-sustained ventricular tachycardia does not predict an adverse
     prognosis
E   cardiac output is usually reduced in severe heart failure

15.10   The following drugs improve prognosis in heart failure:

A   nitrates
B   prazosin
C   hydralazine
D   verapamil
E   nifedipine

15.11   In cardiac failure

A   antidiuretic hormone levels are usually reduced
B   plasma insulin levels are elevated
C   sympathetic activation rarely occurs
D   reverse T3 levels are usually reduced
E   haemoglobin levels rise

15.12   Diuretic therapy

A   may raise serum glucose levels
B   has a recognized association with acute arthritis
C   can lead to a high bicarbonate level
D   usually raises serum magnesium levels
E   induced hyponatraemia should be treated with sodium supplements

15.13 The following are true regarding cardiac transplantation:

A   it is contraindicated if there is a history of previous cardiac surgery
B   it is contraindicated if the pulmonary vascular resistance is greater than 8 Wood units
C   requires HLA-DR antigen matching
D   is contraindicated if there is presensitization to HLA antigens
E   donors must be less than 50 years old

15.14 In the Vaughan Williams classification

A   lignocaine is a class II drug
B   sotalol has class III activity
C   class III agents prolong the action potential
D   digoxin is a class I agent
E   propafenone has class III activity

15.15 Atrial fibrillation

A   can be caused by permanent pacing
B   if paroxysmal has a greater risk of stroke than when persistent
C   should not be treated with calcium channel blockers
D   is associated with a two-fold increased risk of stroke
E   caused by thyrotoxicosis should be cardioverted immediately

15.16 In pre-excitation syndromes

A   a normal QRS complex excludes an accessory pathway
B   atrial fibrillation may cause sudden death
C   the P-R interval is normal in the Lown-Ganong-Levine syndrome
D   tricuspid valve abnormalities are a recognized association
E   accessory pathway conduction becomes slower with advancing age

15.17 In cardiac arrest

A   ventricular fibrillation is associated with a poor prognosis

B   the adrenaline dose administered should not exceed 100 mcg intravenously

C   at least three D-C shocks should be given for ventricular fibrillation before resorting to drug therapy

D   mannitol improves cerebral recovery after cardiac arrest

E   long-term survival after hospital discharge is about 25% at 5 years

15.18 Nitric oxide

A   is a potent vasoconstrictor

B   has a long biological half-life

C   is rapidly inactivated by haemoglobin

D   is produced by endothelial cells

E   production is stimulated by acetylcholine

15.19 Concerning the epidemiology of ischaemic heart disease

A   the annual incidence rate of ischaemic heart disease is over 10 times higher in Finland than in Japan

B   migrants from low-risk countries to high-risk countries continue to be protected from ischaemic heart disease

C   lipoprotein (a) levels are lower in patients with atherosclerosis

D   mortality from ischaemic heart disease has a seasonal variation

E   hormone replacement therapy increases the risk of ischaemic heart disease

15.20 The following are causes of myocardial ischaemia with normal epicardial coronary arteries:

A   infective endocarditis

B   atrial myxoma

C   protein C deficiency

D   hypertrophic cardiomyopathy

E   Syndrome X

15.21 In Takayasu's disease

A   the incidence is greater in males than in females
B   the pulmonary arteries are characteristically unaffected
C   treatment with steroids is effective
D   a retinopathy is well recognized
E   syncope can be a presenting feature

15.22 In hypertrophic cardiomyopathy

A   the genetic mode of transmission is usually autosomal dominant
B   mutation of the gene for cardiac troponin T is well recognized
C   right ventricular hypertrophy is present in over 30%
D   left ventricular hypertrophy increases during adult life
E   the intensity of the ejection systolic murmur is increased by the
     Valsalva manoeuvre

15.23 In systemic lupus erythematosus

A   cardiac involvement is seen in about 20% of patients
B   myocarditis presents with cardiac failure
C   Libman-Sachs endocarditis can occur as an infective complication
D   high titre of antiphospholipid antibodies are associated with
     valvular involvement
E   death from cardiac complications is rare

15.24 In HIV infection

A   the heart is involved in about 50% of patients with AIDS
B   dilated cardiomyopathy is the most common cardiological
     manifestation in the UK
C   dilated cardiomyopathy can be improved by zidovudine
D   isolated right ventricular dilatation can occur
E   cardiac Kaposi's sarcoma causes significant cardiac mortality

15.25 In patients with cyanotic congenital heart disease

A   venesection should always be accompanied by fluid replacement with normal saline
B   there is an increased incidence of arthritis
C   iron deficiency can be present with a normal haemoglobin level
D   pregnancy should be prevented with a high oestrogen contraceptive pill
E   hypertrophic osteoarthropathy can occur

15.26 In Fallot's tetralogy

A   there is overriding of the aorta
B   an associated atrial septal defect is present
C   right heart failure usually occurs in childhood
D   the second heart sound is single
E   can be complicated by aortic regurgitation

15.27 In atrial septal defects

A   ostium secundum defects usually give rise to symptoms in childhood
B   the ECG in ostium secundum defects shows left axis deviation
C   there is a high incidence of atrial fibrillation in later life
D   ostium primum defects are associated with abnormalities of the mitral valve
E   ostium secundum defects are rarer than ostium primum defects

15.28 The following are major criteria for the diagnosis of rheumatic fever:

A   chorea
B   arthralgia
C   erythema marginatum
D   raised ESR
E   subcutaneous nodules

15.29 In rheumatic mitral stenosis

A   a valve area of 1.5 cm² indicates severe stenosis
B   angina can occur
C   splenic infarction does not occur in the absence of endocarditis
D   a short diastolic murmur indicates mild stenosis
E   the signs may be mimicked by cor triatrium

15.30 The following are recognized causes of mitral regurgitation:

A   osteogenesis imperfecta
B   alcohol
C   Marfan's syndrome
D   achondroplasia
E   hypertrophic cardiomyopathy

15.31 Aortic stenosis

A   due to a bicuspid valve usually causes symptoms in childhood
B   predisposes to ventricular arrhythmias
C   may be associated with cannon waves in the jugular venous pulse
D   in association with calcification can be effectively treated with
     balloon valvuloplasty
E   without ECG changes of left ventricular hypertrophy is invariably
     mild

15.32 In aortic regurgitation

A   there is an association with ulcerative colitis
B   there is an association with ventricular septal defect
C   Durosiez's sign represents the nodding of the head in relation to
     the heart beat
D   a short diastolic murmur implies mild regurgitation
E   an ejection systolic murmur usually implies coexistent aortic
     stenosis

15.33 Pulmonary hypertension can be caused by

A high altitude
B pregnancy
C hepatic cirrhosis
D sickle cell disease
E denatured rape seed oil

15.34 Coarctation of the aorta

A most commonly occurs just proximal to the left subclavian artery
B is usually more severe in the post-ductal than in the pre-ductal position
C is more common in males
D has a recognized association with Noonan's syndrome
E when repaired surgically can be complicated by abdominal pain

SECTION 16: INTENSIVE CARE

16.1 **The following statements about the central venous pressure (CVP) are true:**

A introduction of the catheter via the internal jugular vein is preferable to the subclavian approach

B normal venous pressure ranges from +3 to –5 cm of water

C it is possible to have heart failure without a raised venous pressure

D if the CVP is high, an inotropic agent will probably be needed

E if the CVP is low, a plasma expander will probably be needed

16.2 **Positive-pressure ventilation may be indicated in**

A pneumonia

B flail segment of the chest wall

C pulmonary oedema

D cerebral oedema

E low cardiac output

16.3 **The following statements about brain stem function are true:**

A 'doll's head eye movements' occur when long tracts passing through the brain stem from higher centres to the eyes are no longer functioning

B the presence of an abnormally brisk jaw jerk suggests a bilateral, upper motor neurone lesion above the motor nucleus of the Vth cranial nerve

C deviation of both eyes away from an ear irrigated with 50 ml of ice-cold water indicates an intact brain stem

D a positive ciliospinal reflex indicates there are functioning long tracts passing through the length of the brain stem

E the corneal reflexes test the integrity of the VIth cranial nerve

SECTION 17: RESPIRATORY MEDICINE

17.1   Concerning lung structure and function

A   the predominant function of type I cells is the production of
surfactant

B   damaged type I cells are replaced by type II cells

C   high flows are required in the distal airways in order for oxygen to
rapidly diffuse from air to haemoglobin

D   mucociliary clearance is decreased by pollutants and cigarette
smoke

E   surfactant prevents the lung from collapsing at normal
transpulmonary pressures

17.2   Indicate which of the following statements are correct:

A   the VC is greater than the FVC in obstructive ventilatory defects

B   respiratory tract infections leads to an increase in the sputum DNA
content

C   FRC is usually about 50% of the TLC

D   the most effort dependent part of the expiration is shortly before full
expiration

E   the sensitivity of the cough reflex can be assessed by inhaling
capsaicin

17.3   In pneumonia

A   sputum culture is a sensitive method of diagnosing bacterial
pneumonia

B   a positive blood culture is a bad prognostic sign

C   bronchial breathing is the most common clinical finding on
examination

D   *Coxiella burnetti* responds to beta-lactam antibiotics

E   *Mycoplasma* occurs in large epidemics every 3–4 years

17.4   Concerning allergic rhinitis

A   there is an increasing prevalence of seasonal allergic rhinitis due to increasing urban pollen counts

B   maximal symptoms of seasonal allergic rhinitis coincide with maximal grass pollen release

C   the major allergen responsible for perennial allergic rhinitis is Feld-1

D   there is strong evidence for TH2 type cytokine production

E   overdosage with antihistamines used in the treatment of allergic rhinitis is associated with arrhythmias

17.5   Concerning asthma

A   cases arising in adulthood are frequently associated with positive skin tests to common airborne allergens

B   methacholine induces mast cell degranulation in asthmatics

C   beta-2 agonists have no effect on bronchial responsiveness

D   non-allergic (intrinsic) asthmatics do not show the histological appearance seen in allergic asthmatics

E   T-cells are unimportant in the pathogenesis of asthma

17.6   Indicate which of the following statements regarding asthma are correct:

A   airflow obstruction is due principally to large airway smooth muscle contraction

B   it may present with cough and no wheezing

C   exercise-induced asthma is maximal 5–10 minutes after the end of exercise

D   beta-2 agonists can prevent the early response following allergen challenge

E   it is associated with nasal polyps and aspirin intolerance

17.7 Concerning cystic fibrosis (CF)

A   the CF gene is located on the short arm of chromosome 7
B   pneumothorax occurs in about 20% of cases
C   antenatal diagnosis is capable of recognizing all CF chromosomal abnormalities
D   infections can be treated by several classes of oral anti-pseudomonal agents
E   it is associated with asthma

17.8 Indicate which of the following statements regarding bronchiectasis are true:

A   it may be associated with alpha-1 antitrypsin deficiency
B   brain abscesses are a complication
C   *Pseudomonas* species are the most clinically significant causitive organisms
D   the disease is usually localized to a single lobe
E   it may occur with IgG subclass deficiencies

17.9 Indicate which of the following statements regarding chronic obstructive pulmonary disease (COPD) are true:

A   beta-2 agonists are superior to muscarinic antagonists as bronchodilators in COPD
B   weight loss in patients with advanced COPD is usually associated with an underlying neoplasm
C   it is associated with nocturnal desaturation
D   long term oxygen therapy (LTOT) reduces the frequency of admissions
E   a trial of steroids is warranted in patients with COPD

17.10 **Indicate which of the following statements concerning cryptogenic fibrosing alveolitis are correct:**

A   it occurs more frequently in subjects with a history of smoking

B   a ground glass appearance on CT is associated with a better prognosis

C   it is associated with a polyclonal increase in immunoglobulin

D   a high bronchoalveolar lavage (BAL) lymphocyte count is associated with a better response to treatment

E   the response to treatment with azathioprine plus prednisolone is better than prednisolone alone

17.11 **Concerning interstitial lung disease**

A   clubbing is associated with extrinsic allergic alveolitis

B   fibrosing alveolitis does not usually occur before the development of rheumatoid arthritis

C   it may be associated with an elevation in anti-DNA topoisomerase 1 titres

D   asbestosis is normally associated with upper lobe parenchymal shadowing

E   although bronchoalveolar lavage is useful, diagnostic material is rarely obtained in diffuse parenchymal lung disease

17.12 **In asbestos exposure**

A   the latent period for the development of mesothelioma is about 10 years

B   white asbestos (chrysotile) is more hazardous than blue asbestos (crocidolite)

C   there is an association with lipoproteinaceous material obtained at bronchoalveolar lavage

D   pleural plaques are precursors to the development of malignant mesothelioma

E   malignant mesothelioma responds significantly to cytotoxic therapy

17.13 Indicate which of the following statements are correct:

A   constrictive bronchiolitis obliterans responds well to treatment with steroids

B   systemic lupus erythematosus (SLE) may be associated with reduced transdiaphragmatic pressures

C   there is a high incidence of pulmonary hypertension in patients with Sjogren's syndrome

D   ankylosing spondylitis can cause a frozen thorax capable of severe respiratory embarrassment

E   pleural effusion occurring with rheumatoid arthritis is typically an exudate with reduced glucose and pH levels

17.14 Indicate which of the following is associated with positive cANCA titres:

A   Churg Strauss syndrome

B   Goodpasture's syndrome

C   Wegener's granulomatosis

D   bronchocentric granulomatosis

E   microvasculitic polyarteritis nodosa

17.15 Indicate which of the following is associated with pulmonary eosinophilia:

A   polyarteritis nodosa

B   Lofgren's syndrome

C   allergic bronchopulmonary aspergillosis

D   extrinsic allergic alveolitis

E   sarcoidosis

17.16 Extrinsic allergic alveolitis

A   is due to a type III hypersensitivity reaction
B   usually requires open lung biopsy to make a diagnosis
C   is usually caused by inhalation of *Aspergillus fumigatus* from mouldy hay
D   is a granulomatous disorder of the lung
E   is characterized by symptoms typically appearing 6–9 hours after exposure to the allergen

17.17 Indicate which of the following regarding sarcoidosis is correct:

A   there is a predominance of CD 8 bearing cells
B   it is associated with cutaneous anergy
C   it may be associated with VII nerve palsy
D   cardiac involvement usually takes the form of valvular lesions
E   it is associated with a polyclonal increase in immunoglobulins

17.18 Indicate which of the following statements regarding lung cancer are true:

A   hypercalcemia is usually associated with ectopic parathormone secretion by squamous cell carcinomas
B   pneumonectomy should not be undertaken if the patient cannot sustain a FEV_1 of more than 1.2l
C   elderly patients tolerate lobectomy as well as young patients
D   superior vena caval (SVC) obstruction should usually be treated with radiotherapy
E   the TNM classification is useful in the staging and of prognostic value in small cell lung cancer

17.19 In respiratory failure

A   V/Q abnormalities are the major mechanism of hypoxia in most patients with lung disease

B   the arterial-alveolar gradient is a good measure of ventilatory capacity

C   hypercapnia causes increased intracranial pressure

D   obstructive sleep apnoea is associated with type 2 respiratory failure

E   chronic hypoxia can lead to lethargy, mental slowing and confusion

17.20 In obstructive sleep apnoea

A   there is an association with nocturnal bradycardia

B   oronasal factors are unimportant

C   tricyclic antidepressants may worsen the symptoms

D   there is a reduced arousal response in REM sleep

E   the polysomnograph typically shows thoracoabdominal movement paradox

17.21 Concerning lung transplantation

A   one-year survival after transplantation is about 80%

B   double lung transplantation is suitable for primary pulmonary hypertension

C   obliterative bronchiolitis accounts for most of the long-term deaths after transplantation

D   recipients require higher immunosuppressive doses of cyclosporin compared with recipients of other organs

E   cytomegalovirus (CMV) can be acquired from the donor

SECTION 18: RHEUMATOLOGY

18.1   The following are commonly found in reactive arthritis:

A   enthesitis
B   alopecia
C   oral ulceration
D   scleritis
E   keratoderma blennorrhagica

18.2   Rheumatoid arthritis

A   typically affects peripheral joints
B   has a peak incidence in the years 20–30
C   develops insidiously over weeks or months in most patients
D   affects males and females equally
E   causes destruction of articular cartilage

18.3   The following facts about gout are true:

A   the first acute attack of gout usually resolves spontaneously over
     5–15 days if left untreated
B   most hyperuricaemic people will never develop gout
C   men and women with ischaemic heart disease have an increased
     chance of developing gout
D   most patients with primary gout are undersecretors of uric acid
E   the treatment of choice is allopurinol except in elderly patients in
     whom there are frequent side-effects

18.4   In septic arthritis

A   haematogenous spread of organisms from a remote site is more
     common than a local cause for the infection
B   malignancy is a predisposing factor
C   *Staphylococcus aureus* is the most likely causative organism in
     children under 2 years of age
D   the ankle is the most commonly affected joint
E   intra-articular antibiotics are indicated in severe infections

18.5   Arthritis is a recognized feature of the following conditions:

A   measles
B   mumps
C   hepatitis B
D   coccidioidomycosis
E   trichomonas vaginalis

**18.6   Rapidly progressive glomerulonephritis is a recognized feature of
the following conditions:**

A   systemic lupus erythematosus
B   polymyositis
C   polyarteritis
D   giant-cell arteritis
E   Wegener's granulomatosis

18.7   The following facts about giant-cell arteritis are true:

A   presentation before the age of 50 is rare
B   the onset of symptoms is usually insidious over months, even a year
C   temporal artery biopsy is the definitive test
D   recurrence after successful treatment is very rare
E   there is no reduction in life expectancy

18.8 **Chemical agents implicated in the development of scleroderma include**

    A   rubber
    B   asbestos
    C   silica
    D   silicone
    E   cocaine

18.9 **The recognized features of systemic lupus erythematosus include**

    A   keloid scarring
    B   nephritis
    C   Raynaud's phenomenon
    D   thrombocytopenia
    E   pulmonary atelectasis

SECTION 19: DISORDERS OF THE SKELETON

19.1   Osteoblasts

    A   are derived from the haemopoietic system
    B   synthesize collagen
    C   control bone mineralization
    D   appear to direct the activity of other bony cells
    E   are activated by parathyroid hormone

19.2   Low fasting plasma phosphate concentrations are found in

    A   hypoparathyroidism
    B   hypercalcaemia of malignancy
    C   renal glomerular failure
    D   inherited rickets
    E   prolonged intravenous nutrition

19.3   The following increase the rate of bone loss:

    A   smoking
    B   early menarche
    C   excess body weight
    D   alcohol
    E   immobility

19.4   The recognized features of osteomalacia include:

    A   painless bowing of the long bones
    B   triradiate pelvis
    C   vertebral collapse
    D   proximal muscle weakness
    E   bossing of the frontal and parietal bones

19.5 In Paget's disease

A only about 50% of patients are symptomatic at presentation
B osteosarcoma occurs in about one in six patients
C deafness is one of the few symptoms which can be successfully treated
D plasma acid phosphatase levels are a good indicator of response to treatment
E many patients require no treatment

19.6 The following are recognized features of type I osteogenesis imperfecta:

A Looser's zones
B increased incidence of lower limb fractures
C significant scoliosis
D aortic incompetence
E blue sclerae

19.7 The following statements about these congenital conditions affecting the skeleton are true:

A mitral valve prolapse occurs in osteogenesis imperfecta
B aortic stenosis occurs in Marfan's syndrome
C thromboembolism is a common feature of homocystinuria
D abnormal cerebrovascular supply leading to mental retardation occurs in achondroplasia
E mucopolysaccharide deposits induce coronary artery disease in Hurler's syndrome

SECTION 20: NEPHROLOGY

20.1   When analysing a sample of urine

A   microalbuminuria can be qualitatively estimated by standard dipstick

B   the presence of nitrites suggests urinary infection

C   glomerular bleeding is characterized by over 70% dysmorphic erythrocytes

D   the Tamm-Horsfall mucoprotein enters the urine by glomerular filtration

E   hyaline casts are indicative of a pathological state

20.2   Concerning renal imaging

A   the fatality rate associated with IVU is about 0.001%

B   venography is the most appropriate technique for detecting renal vein thrombosis

C   ultrasound should be the first line radiological investigation of both acute and chronic renal failure

D   MAG 3 is the first choice radionuclide for identifying renal scars

E   captopril renography is too insensitive for the detection of functionally significant renal artery stenosis

20.3   The following support a diagnosis of psychogenic polydipsia rather than cranial diabetes insipidus:

A   a history of abrupt onset

B   a plasma osmolality of 265 mOsmol/kg

C   24-hour urine output of 8–12 litres

D   absence of nocturnal polyuria

E   a urine osmolality of 700 mOsmol/kg after a water deprivation test

20.4 In patients with nephrotic syndrome

A   ACE inhibitors will lead to a similar proportionate decrement in both proteinuria and GFR
B   salt restriction is more valuable than water restriction
C   low serum IgG is an important cause of susceptibility to infection
D   adults are particularly vulnerable to pneumococcal infection
E   the prevalence of renal vein thrombosis is about 10%

20.5 The following glomerular conditions usually present with haematuria:

A   Henoch-Schönlein nephritis
B   thin-membrane nephropathy
C   Goodpasture's syndrome
D   membranous nephropathy
E   mesangiocapillary glomerulonephritis (MCGN)

20.6 Minimal-change nephropathy

A   is associated with Hodgkin's lymphoma
B   does not relapse after remission
C   produces highly-selective proteinuria in most adults
D   rarely progresses to end-stage renal failure
E   may have a genetic predisposition

20.7 Rapidly progressive glomerulonephritis

A   may occur in systemic lupus erythematosus (SLE)
B   is usually accompanied by crescentic change in renal biopsy
C   can be associated with anti-glomerular basement membrane antibodies which are pathogenic
D   should be treated with high dose immunosuppression
E   will preclude future renal transplantation

20.8 **The following are true of patients with diabetic nephropathy:**

A   they constitute 30% of patients treated with renal replacement therapy

B   the mortality is less than in patients with other forms of nephropathy

C   the prevalence of proteinuria is comparable in type I and type 2 diabetics for any given duration of the diabetic disease

D   once proteinuria is established no therapeutic strategies can ameliorate the decline towards renal failure

E   hypertriglyceridaemia is the most common dyslipidaemia in the uraemic diabetic patient

20.9 **Nephropathy has a well-recognized association with the following infections:**

A   *Staphylococcus epidermidis*

B   *Salmonella typhi*

C   Legionnaire's disease

D   hepatitis A

E   Hanta virus

20.10 **Concerning vesico-ureteric reflux (VUR)**

A   micturating cystourethrography is the most precise imaging technique to demonstrate VUR

B   DTPA scanning is considered preferable to intravenous urogram in demonstrating renal scarring

C   urinary tract infections are the commonest manifestation of VUR in infants and children

D   familial inheritance of VUR is well-recognized

E   if VUR is identified in adults, surgical correction may be indicated

20.11 In analgesic nephropathy

A   urinary sodium excretion is often low
B   the intravenous urogram appearances are often distinguishable from reflux nephropathy
C   nephrocalcinosis may be present
D   persistent microscopic haematuria is probably due to papillary necrosis
E   renal biopsy will establish the diagnosis

20.12 Treatment with the following drugs may be associated with development of proteinuria:

A   gentamicin
B   penicillamine
C   lithium
D   cisplatin
E   tetracycline

20.13 The following drugs should be used in reduced dosage in patients with severe renal failure:

A   amoxycillin
B   erythromycin
C   allopurinol
D   rifampicin
E   cimetidine

20.14 Following a road traffic accident a patient sustains multiple injuries and develops oliguria. The following would be compatible with acute tubular necrosis:

A   plasma bicarbonate of 10 mmol/l
B   fractional excretion of sodium of 0.5%
C   urine osmolality of 900 mOsmol/kg
D   serum calcium of 1.9 mmol/l
E   urine/plasma creatinine ratio of 1:10

20.15 In patients with nephropathy associated with multiple myeloma

   A   the clinical pattern of renal disease is predicted by the physico-chemical properties of the particular light chains

   B   'fractured' intra-tubular casts are typical

   C   recovery from renal failure should be anticipated in the majority of cases

   D   a one-year survival of <10% is expected when dialysis becomes necessary

   E   hyperuricaemia does not require treatment

20.16 The following factors would favour a choice of haemodialysis rather than continuous ambulatory peritoneal dialysis in managing a patient with end-stage renal failure:

   A   residual renal function of 4 ml/min

   B   polycystic kidney disease

   C   co-existent malnutrition

   D   active psychotic disorder

   E   recurrent herniae

20.17 When contemplating transplantation in a patient with chronic renal failure

   A   cadaveric transplantation should not occur until the patient has remained stable on dialysis for 3 months

   B   generalized bronchiectasis precludes transplantation

   C   amyloidosis precludes transplantation

   D   preferential HLA matching at the A, rather than the B, locus is more important for graft prognosis

   E   blood transfusion in the pre-transplantation phase is widely recommended

20.18 **For a patient who has had a successful renal transplant the following are true:**

A   erythrocytosis is a recognized finding
B   non-Hodgkin's lymphoma is the likeliest malignancy to develop
C   if the patient develops hypertension, orthodox drug therapy will probably be ineffective
D   sepsis is the leading cause of death
E   a glomerular filtration rate of 30–40 ml/min may be expected

20.19 **Concerning renal bone disease**

A   radiography is a sensitive means of assessment
B   vascular calcification is often associated
C   bone biopsy is necessary for diagnosis of aluminium-related bone disease
D   hyperparathyroidism should usually be treated by parathyroidectomy
E   hypercalcaemia is common after renal transplantation

20.20 **The following are true of renal tubular acidosis (RTA):**

A   renal stone formation occurs in RTA-1
B   hypokalaemia occurs in all types of RTA
C   primary RTA-1 is an autosomal dominant disorder
D   RTA-2 is associated with aminoaciduria
E   oral bicarbonate requirement is greater in RTA-2 than RTA-1

21.1 **The following facts about sexually transmitted diseases (STDs) are true:**

A   gonorrhoea is still the most common STD presenting at UK specialist clinics

B   in the UK, syphilis continues to decline in frequency

C   the frequency rates for STDs overall are higher in developing than in developed countries

D   trichomoniasis is the most common STD worldwide

E   heterosexual transmission of AIDS in developing countries is more common than homosexual transmission

21.2 **In genital herpes**

A   the first attack lasts about 20 days

B   the first attack is more painful in men than in women

C   complications rarely occur in the first attack

D   the neonatal form has about a 50–60% mortality

E   recurrent attacks are usually longer and more severe than the first

21.3 **Bacterial vaginosis**

A   is caused by gardnerella

B   is characterized by intense vaginal wall inflammation

C   is characterized by an unpleasant odour and persistent pruritus

D   is commonly treated with metronidazole

E   rarely recurs following successful treatment

SECTION 22: BLOOD

22.1 Acute myeloblastic leukaemia

A   mostly affects young adults
B   usually arises from a pluripotent stem cell
C   presents with circulating myeloblasts containing Auer rods in most cases
D   of the M5 (monocytic) sub-type is associated with the t(15;17) translocation and a coagulopathy at presentation
E   in children has a higher remission rate after treatment than in adults

22.2 In acute lymphoblastic leukaemia (ALL)

A   in childhood the cure rate is about 90% with modern treatment regimens
B   there may be pre-existing Fanconi's syndrome
C   hyperdiploidy with more than 50 chromosomes per cell is the cytogenic abnormality associated with the best prognosis
D   maintenance treatment of 1–2 years after remission induction gives the best result
E   during maintenance therapy, continuous co-trimoxazole therapy is important to prevent cryptococcal infection

22.3 Paroxysmal nocturnal haemoglobinuria (PNH) is a condition which

A   seldom affects cell lineages other than the erythroid series
B   may present with massive haematuria
C   may present with iron deficiency anaemia
D   may need long term warfarin treatment because venous thrombosis is a recognized cause of death in this condition
E   may need treatment with cyclical chemotherapy regimens

22.4 **The following statements relate to human iron metabolism:**

A   90% of total body iron in health is in the form of haemoglobin

B   iron in green leafy vegetables is well absorbed and a major source of dietary iron

C   iron excretion is predominantly in the faeces

D   serum iron is a useful measure of iron supply to the tissues

E   transferrin saturation above 50% is needed to maintain normal erythropoiesis

22.5 **In iron overload**

A   due to hereditary haemochromatosis, the marked male preponderance in presentation occurs because it is a sex-linked condition

B   due to hereditary haemochromatosis, hypogonadism in males results from testicular iron deposition

C   due to hereditary haemochromatosis, treatment by venesection should aim to keep the haemoglobin below 15 g/dl

D   due to hereditary haemochromatosis, hepatocellular carcinoma is a common cause of death

E   secondary to regular blood transfusion in thalassaemia major, treatment with desferrioxamine should be started between the ages of 6–10 years

22.6 **Vitamin B12 deficiency**

A   due to pernicious anaemia (PA) is characterized by parietal cell antibodies and intrinsic factor antibodies although both also occur in subjects with atrophic gastritis without PA

B   due to PA carries a three-fold increased risk of gastric carcinoma

C   may occur without any anaemia in patients with severe symmetrical neuropathy

D   is much more frequent in HIV infected individuals than controls

E   due to dietary deficiency can be treated with 50 mcg of oral hydroxycobalamin daily

22.8   The following statements are true about the thalassaemias:

A   the thalassaemias are inherited in a Mendelian co-dominant
     fashion
B   beta thalassaemia trait is common in South East Asia
C   beta thalassaemia normally arises from deletion of the genes
D   in beta thalassaemia major patients who are well transfused from
     infancy, bony changes and marked splenomegaly are rare
E   the chain production of a single alpha gene, where the other three
     are thalassaemic and failing to contribute any useful chain
     production, is compatible with survival into adult life with
     relatively few health problems

22.8   In sickle cell anaemia (haemoglobin SS)

A   jaundice is an indication that the patient is in crisis
B   splenomegaly is frequently found in childhood
C   parvovirus may cause an acute haemolytic crisis
D   profound anaemia may occur as blood is trapped or 'sequestered' in
     a suddenly enlarged liver or spleen
E   gallstones occur in up to one-third of affected individuals by their
     late teens

22.9   Methaemoglobinaemia

A   results from an unstable haemoglobin
B   may occur because of a low level of NADH-diaphorase or from
     certain alpha or beta globin chain structural variants
C   causes polycythaemia
D   causes cyanosis
E   can be caused, in its acquired form, by sulphonamide
     administration

22.10 In sideroblastic anaemia

A   there is hypochromia of the red cells, with iron loading of the red cell marrow precursors

B   of the primary acquired type, the condition can evolve into leukaemia

C   a dimorphic blood film is seen

D   macrocytosis is often seen in the primary acquired type

E   there is frequently a useful response to oral pyridoxine

22.11 The following statements are true of red cell breakdown, or haemolysis:

A   the process is reflected by rising haptoglobin

B   there is increased production of faecal and urinary urobilinogen

C   the normal half-life of Cr^{51} labelled own red cells (time for half of label to disappear from circulation) is 60 days, reduced in haemolysis

D   when due to hereditary spherocytosis can be attributed to membrane lipid abnormalities

E   due to hereditary spherocytosis is mostly inherited in an autosomal dominant manner

22.12 Glucose-6-phosphate dehydrogenase (G6PD) deficiency

A   is sex linked so female carriers are unaffected

B   in the majority of affected individuals gives no clinical problems throughout their lives

C   can give rise to neonatal jaundice indistinguishable from that caused by Rhesus incompatibility

D   may give rise to a chronic non-spherocytic haemolytic anaemia

E   after an acute haemolytic episode, commonly gives rise to Howell-Jolly bodies on the blood film

22.13 Microangiopathic haemolytic anaemia

A   always occurs in association with coagulation deficiencies

B   gives a blood film in which spherocytes are usually seen

C   often responds to oral corticosteroids

D   due to haemolytic uraemic syndrome has been associated with
    E. coli infection

E   in thrombotic thrombocytopenia purpura (TTP) there may be
    abnormal release from endothelium of high molecular weight Von
    Willebrand multimers

22.14 The following statements relate to polycythaemia:

A   in polycythaemia rubra vera a raised platelet count is commonly
    associated

B   secondary polycythaemia occurs due to reduced plasma volume

C   if associated with a reduced haemoglobin P_{50} (left shift of the
    oxygen dissociation curve) may be due to smoking

D   when the packed cell volume (PCV) exceeds 0.48 (48%) there may
    be a significant decrease in cerebral blood flow

E   polycythaemia may result from low affinity haemoglobin variants

22.15 The following statements are true of human leucocyte biology:

A   all granulocytes (neutrophils, eosinophils, basophils) arise from
    bone marrow myeloblasts

B   all granulocytes are phagocytic

C   mature neutrophils stay in the peripheral circulation for up to
    3 days

D   a neutrophil count of less than $1.5 \times 10^9/l$ may be found in healthy
    people from black or Arab populations

E   the storage pool of neutrophils, where they remain before entering
    the circulation, may contain up to 15 times the number of cells
    found in the peripheral blood

22.16 Lymph nodes

A which become enlarged due to malignancy may be tender or painful

B in health contain small follicular cells in the germinal centres, also known as centrocytes or small-cleaved cells

C may be enlarged in individuals with Addison's disease

D which are enlarged in infectious mononucleosis show marked paracortical (T-cell) expansion.

E which are enlarged because of lymphoma are more commonly due to Hodgkin's disease than non-Hodgkin's lymphoma

22.17 The following statements are true of Hodgkin's disease:

A the affected nodes may fluctuate in size or shrink spontaneously

B if the spleen is enlarged it is involved with disease histologically

C systemic symptoms of fever, night sweats and weight loss affect a minority of patients

D radiotherapy alone is frequently curative

E it may relapse after treatment into a type of non-Hodgkin's lymphoma

22.18 Prognosis in Hodgkin's disease

A is adversely affected by a low lymphocyte count at presentation

B is favourably affected by eosinophilia

C is better in those patients who have been fully histologically staged by laparotomy and splenectomy

D is poorer in those with bulky mediastinal disease of nodular sclerosing histology than other presentations with the same histology

E is currently such that 70–80% of patients survive to 5 years

22.19 In non-Hodgkin's lymphoma

A spread to extra-nodal areas is much commoner than in Hodgkin's disease

B of Burkett sub-type, a translocation between chromosome 8 and 14 is characteristic

C 'MALT' derived tumours in the stomach may show response to antibiotic treatment aimed at eradicating *H. pylori*

D the presence or absence of systemic symptoms is an important prognostic indicator

E cure is rare in tumours of low grade histology

22.20 The spleen

A is the major site of lymphopoiesis in infants

B is responsible for removing Howell–Jolly bodies and Heinz bodies from red cells

C contains around 20% of the body's total lymphoid pool

D normally contains less than 5% of the total body red cell mass

E has to be enlarged to more than 3 times normal size before it is palpable

22.21 Splenic enlargement

A needs to be massive before hypersplenism is seen

B causes neutropenia less commonly than anaemia or thrombocytopenia

C can be associated with increased plasma volume or hypervolaemia, if enlargement is marked

D when due to tropical splenomegaly may respond to long-term anti-malarial treatment with sustained reduction in spleen size

E can cause splenic rupture in non-malignant as well as malignant conditions

22.22 In myeloma

A   circulating plasma cells can frequently be seen on the peripheral blood film before treatment

B   infections with Gram-positive, Gram-negative and opportunistic infections, such as *Mycobacterium tuberculosis*, are greatly increased

C   about 60% of patients have skeletal lytic lesions at presentation, a further 20% have osteoporosis alone

D   prognosis is influenced by Beta 2 microglobulin level at presentation

E   interferon-alpha treatment defers relapse after initial treatment to plateau phase

22.23 Waldenstrom's macroglobulinaemia

A   is the commonest cause of IgM paraproteinaemia

B   usually presents with peripheral lymphocytosis

C   hyperviscosity syndrome, common at presentation, may cause visual disturbances and pathological bleeding

D   where hyperviscosity is a problem, it may be treated with plasmapheresis which is effective in this disease because 90% of IgM is intravascular

E   commonly causes bone lesions late in the disease course

22.24 Immune thrombocytopenic purpura (ITP)

A   results from antibody binding to platelet surface antigens and reducing platelet survival from the usual span of around 5 days

B   frequently causes an enlarged spleen, detectable at presentation

C   is more frequently found in people with HIV infection than in the general population

D   in the history of a pregnant woman is an indication for careful monitoring of mother and baby, because neonatal thrombocytopenia can occur even in the presence of a normal maternal platelet count

E   responds to oral steroids after 2–3 weeks in two-thirds of patients

22.25 Haemophilia A

A   arises because of a spontaneous mutation in about 30% of patients
B   is more likely to be accompanied by factor VIII inhibitor formation
if caused by gene deletion than other mutations
C   may cause different levels of factor VIII deficiency, and so clinical
disease severity, in affected individuals within the same kindred
D   rarely gives spontaneous major problems unless the procoagulant factor
VIII (factor VIII:C) level is less than 1/dl (less than 1% of normal)
E   is rarely usefully treated with DDAVP

**22.26 The following statements are true of inherited coagulation factor
deficiencies:**

A   for treatment of factor IX deficiency (Christmas disease) DDAVP
is ineffective and it is now recommended that high purity IX
concentrate is used for treatment of these patients
B   homozygous factor XI deficiency gives a severe bleeding disorder
with spontaneous haemorrhage such as is seen in the haemophilias
C   factor XII deficiency may predispose to thromboses
D   factor VII deficiency can give a severe bleeding disorder with
spontaneous haemorrhages such as is seen in the haemophilias
E   patients with severe factor V deficiency may have a prolonged
bleeding time

22.27 A hypercoagulable state

A   is now felt to be most commonly due to an inherited defect in the
natural anticoagulant mechanisms
B   due to antithrombin III deficiency is inherited in an autosomal
dominant fashion
C   due to antithrombin III deficiency classically gives venous and
arterial thrombotic events
D   due to protein C deficiency will cause symptoms in 80% of
affected individuals by the age of 40
E   due to activated protein C resistance is attributed to a point
mutation in the factor V gene, and this may be a cause in a large
number of individuals with thromboses

22.28 Blood transfusion reactions

A   of the delayed haemolytic type may occur even if there is a negative pre-transfusion antibody screen

B   due to HLA antibodies can only be avoided by freezing/washing red cell to remove leucocytes

C   due to HLA antibodies can cause high fevers, rigors, and haemoglobinuria soon after the transfusion commences

D   of a severe allergic type may result from formation of anti-IgA antibodies in an individual who is IgA deficient

E   can be avoided by meticulous cross-matching of red cells prior to transfusion

22.29 The following statements relate to complications of allogeneic bone marrow transplantation:

A   acute graft versus host disease may be seen at any time up to 3 months after transplant, and is caused by tissue damage by donor cytotoxic T-cells

B   removal of T-cells from the donor marrow reduces the risk of graft versus host disease and decreases the risk of graft rejection and leukaemic relapse

C   interstitial pneumonitis is frequently attributable to cytomegalovirus infection

D   fractionated total body irradiation to a higher total dose than single fraction irradiation as conditioning, reduces the risk of subsequent leukaemic relapse

E   in children, reduced growth velocity is seen after total body irradiation, but not chemotherapeutic conditioning alone

SECTION 23: SKIN

23.1 **The following facts about the structure of the skin are true:**

A   the pigmentary cells, the melanocytes, are found within the dermis F

B   vasodilation can increase skin blood flow by up to twice normal blood flow   +

C   basal cells are responsible for producing keratin T

D   the epidermis replaces itself completely about once every 30 days T

E   the skin can synthesize vitamin D from calciferol in the presence of sunlight T

23.2 **The following dermatological terms are accurately described:**

A   a macule is a soft elevation of the epidermis or dermis of no particular shape or content   F

B   a papule is a circumscribed, firm elevation or thickening of the epidermis or upper dermis usually caused by oedema

C   a plaque is a flat lesion of indeterminate shape and edge characterized by a change in skin colour   F

D   a nodule is a well defined palpable mass greater than 1 cm in diameter and usually consisting of oedema, inflammatory or malignant cells filling the dermis or subcutaneous tissue   F

E   a vesicle is a visible accumulation of fluid less than 1 cm in diameter   T

23.3 **Severe pain on compression of the following tumours is a well recognized symptom:**

A   leiomyoma

B   rhabdomyoma

C   neuroma

D   osteoma

E   glomus tumour

23.4 The following abnormalities are not inherited:

A   accessory nipple
B   Dupuytren's contracture
C   webbed neck
D   accessory digits
E   hypoplastic toenails

23.5 The following conditions have an autosomal dominant inheritance:

A   neurofibromatosis
B   phenylketonuria
C   oculocutaneous albinism
D   Peut–Jeghers syndrome
E   ichthyosis vulgaris

23.6 The following gastrointestinal conditions are linked to the following dermatological signs:

A   gastric atrophy and vitiligo F
B   Crohn's disease and erythema nodosum T
C   coeliac disease with acanthosis nigricans T
D   gastric carcinoma with dermatitis herpetiformis T
E   Whipple's disease and pigmentation

23.7 The following substances are recognized causes of contact dermatitis:

A   nickel in earrings T
B   formaldehyde in perfumes T
C   mercury in false teeth T
D   rubber in tights T
E   acrylic in spectacle frames

23.8 The recognized causes of pruritus include

A iron deficiency
B acute renal failure
C polycythaemia
D hyperthyroidism
E carcinoma of the pancreas

23.9 In psoriasis

A there is about a tenfold increase in the speed of epidermal proliferation
B the lesion-free skin in affected patients is normal
C lesions may develop in traumatized skin
D arthropathy occurs in about one-third of affected patients
E the application of local steroid creams and ointments should be avoided

23.10 The recognized features of lichen planus include

A violaceous papules
B patches of hypopigmentation
C Wickham striae
D alopecia
E telangiectasia

23.11 The histological features of acne vulgaris include

A an increase in the number of sebaceous glands
B an increase in the size of sebaceous glands
C an increase in the amount of sebum produced
D blockage of the pilosebaceous ducts
E increased lipogenesis due to increased androgen activity

23.12 The following statements about vitiligo are true:

A   there is an association with autoimmune diseases
B   the principal affected cell is the keratinocyte
C   vitiligo is rare in children under 10 years of age
D   affected sites appear randomly selected with no link or symmetry
E   depigmentation of the lesion is usually total

23.13 The following statements about hair are true:

A   the foetal lanugo hair is shed into the amniotic fluid
B   each hair grows at the rate of about 1 cm per month
C   about 50–300 hairs are shed each day from the scalp
D   the eyelashes may lengthen in the course of chronic liver disease
E   it is a myth that a shock may cause a person to lose hair at a greatly accelerated rate

23.14 The following facts about urticaria are true:

A   almost all urticaria is allergic
B   urticaria does not appear to have a genetic basis
C   about one-quarter of cases of acute hepatitis present with urticaria
D   no cause is found in most adult cases of chronic urticaria
E H_2-blockers have replaced H_1-blockers as the treatment of choice for chronic urticaria

23.15 Pyoderma gangrenosum may occur in association with

A   myeloma
B   leukaemia
C   venous stasis
D   Behçet's disease
E   rheumatoid arthritis

SECTION 24: NEUROLOGY

24.1 **The following are correctly matched:**

A   hemineglect and temporal lobe lesions
B   acalculia and parietal lobe lesions
C   recent memory impairment and parietal lobe lesions
D   verbal memory problems and temporal lobe lesions
E   Wernicke's aphasia and fluent speech

24.2 **With regard to the visual pathways**

A   demyelination of the optic nerve often causes loss of colour vision
B   a lesion at the optic chiasm may cause an upper temporal quadrantanopia opposite to a central scotoma
C   lesions of the optic tract are usually secondary to trauma
D   damage to the optic radiation in the parietal lobe will cause an inferior bitemporal hemianopia
E   occipital lesions may cause prosopagnosia

24.3 **With nystagmus**

A   the direction is specified by the direction of the slow phase
B   if the fast phase is to the right, right sided vestibular damage may be suspected
C   gaze evoked nystagmus may be induced by cerebellar lesions
D   up-beat nystagmus may occur in lesions of the medial longitudinal bundle
E   rotational nystagmus is associated with syringomyelia

24.4   The following are true with regard to cerebellar pontine angle tumours:

A   the majority are meningiomas
B   Schwannomas are more frequent in neurofibromatosis type I
C   presentation is often with earache or headache
D   gadolinium enhanced magnetic resonance imaging (MRI) is the investigation of choice
E   radiotherapy is the treatment of choice in most patients

24.5   The following statements are true:

A   the oculomotor nerve (III) is responsible for depression of the adducted eye
B   the oculomotor nerve supplies most muscle fibres responsible for eyelid elevation
C   cavernous sinus aneurysms may cause complete ophthalmoplegia
D   anisocoria is common with bilateral Argyll Robertson pupils (ARPs)
E   the third division of the trigeminal nerve supplies skin over the angle of the jaw

24.6   Trigeminal neuralgia

A   is usually characterized by lancinating pain
B   treatment with carbamazepine usually causes significant side effects therefore decreasing its use
C   may be an early feature of multiple sclerosis
D   may be triggered by cold air
E   may give rise to significant weight loss

24.7 In testing autonomic function

A   absence of sinus arrhythmia on deep breathing indicates vagal afferent dysfunction

B   carotid sinus massage may decrease cardiac rate

C   the blood pressure fall during the Valsalva manoeuvre is lost in peripheral sympathetic lesion

D   2.5% cocaine has no effect on a sympathetically denervated pupil

E   2.5% methacholine causes constriction after parasympathetic denervation

24.8 In spinal cord disease:

A   a root lesion at L5 would abolish the knee reflex

B   subacute combined degeneration of the cord (SACD) may cause significant demyelination of the white matter

C   severe SACD may occur without anaemia

D   syringomyelia may cause a 'dissociated' sensory loss

E   tumours are most often extrinsic

24.9 In epilepsy

A   myoclonic jerks are partial seizures

B   absence seizures are generalized

C   3 per second spike and wave activity is usual in complex partial seizures

D   20% of epilepsies are thought to be inherited

E   a UK driving licence may be revoked after the first unprovoked seizure

24.10 In narcolepsy

A there is an association with HLA DR2
B sleep onset REM may occur
C a UK driving licence may be withdrawn
D sleep paralysis occurs in approximately 50% of patients
E clomipramine may improve daytime sleepiness

24.11 With regard to the cerebral circulation and cerebrovascular disease

A the ophthalmic artery is a branch of the anterior cerebral artery
B the dura is supplied from both internal and external carotid arteries
C a lacunar infarct may result in a pure sensory stroke
D a left hemisphere infarct may cause the head to turn to the right
E a total anterior circulation infarction (TACI) causes homonymous hemianopia

24.12 In dementias

A Alzheimer's disease is predominantly a cortical dementia
B slowing of cognitive processes is typical of Alzheimer's disease
C Creutzfeldt-Jakob disease usually causes severe memory impairment
D Huntington's disease is characterized by poor attention
E Parkinson's disease is a cause of cortical dementia

24.13 In Friedreich's ataxia

A inheritance is autosomal recessive
B there is loss of dorsal root ganglion cells
C cerebellar disease causes nystagmus in most cases
D pupillary reactions are slowed due to brainstem demyelination
E electrocardiography will be abnormal in the majority of cases

24.14 In the neurocutaneous syndromes

A   the gene for neurofibromatosis (NF) type I is on chromosome 17
B   tuberous sclerosis is characterized by epilepsy
C   most cases of tuberous sclerosis have a positive family history
D   cerebelloretinal haemangioblastosis (Von Hippel-Lindau disease) is
     associated with megaloblastic anaemia
E   ataxia-telangiectasia is associated with immunoglobulin deficiency

24.15 In multiple sclerosis

A   the onset is progressive in about 10%
B   benign disease is more common in males
C   incoordination is associated with a poor prognosis
D   more than 90% of patients have periventricular lesions
     demonstrated by magnetic resonance imaging
E   oligoclonal bands in the CSF and serum strongly support the diagnosis

24.16 In Wilson's disease

A   all patients have deficiency of ceruloplasmin
B   dementia is a common first symptom
C   absence of Kayser-Fleischer (KF) rings in a patient with dysarthria
     would suggest an alternative diagnosis
D   liver and neurological disease usually coexist
E   the globus pallidus and putamen are markedly affected

24.17 The following are true about migraine:

A   migraine with aura is more common than migraine without aura
B   it most commonly starts before the age of 30
C   if hemiparesis develops embolisation from the ipsilateral carotid
     artery is most likely
D   sumatriptan is a 5-HT$_1$ agonist
E   remission is common during pregnancy

24.18 With regard to meningitis

A   *E. coli* is a common cause in the neonate
B   *H. influenzae* is decreasing as a cause in children
C   *N. meningitides* and *Strep. pneumoniae* account for 85% of adult cases
D   a CSF lymphocytosis may occur in bacterial meningitis
E   post-traumatic meningitis should be treated as a community acquired meningitis

24.19 With human immunodeficiency virus type I (HIV I)

A   aseptic meningitis is a common neurological manifestation of the primary infection illness
B   a painful proximal myopathy may occur during the stage of asymptomatic infection
C   a peripheral neuropathy may be detected in more than 80% of patients with AIDS
D   cryptococcal meningitis usually produces a chronic illness
E   Kaposi's sarcoma metastasises to the CNS in about 50%

24.20 The following are true:

A   if the ulnar nerve is damaged at the wrist, sensation over the little finger is impaired
B   if the median nerve is damaged at the elbow there will be weakness of supination
C   a radial nerve lesion in the axilla will cause impairment of grip
D   the anterior interosseous nerve is a branch of the radial nerve
E   a posterior interosseous nerve lesion will cause weakness of the extensor carpi ulnaris

SECTION 25: DISORDERS OF THE VOLUNTARY MUSCLES

25.1   In Duchenne muscular dystrophy

A   only boys are affected
B   the disease usually becomes apparent in the early adolescent years
C   high serum creatine kinase levels are characteristic
D   treatment with steroids markedly improves symptoms for an initial period of 2–3 years
E   many patients now survive into their late twenties

25.2   The recognized features of dystrophia myotonia include:

A   pseudohypertrophy of forearm and calf muscles
B   cardiac valvular abnormalities
C   ptosis
D   impotence
E   mental retardation

25.3   In myasthenia gravis

A   the disease process usually spares the ocular muscles
B   the development of antibodies to the acetylcholine receptor in muscle is considered to be the cause in most cases
C   the pituitary may show abnormal histological changes
D   weakness of skeletal muscle increases with exercise
E   treatment with plasma exchange is no longer recommended

SECTION 26: THE EYE

26.1 In the red eye

A   conjunctivitis is a likely diagnosis if there is an accompanying
    sticky discharge
B   episcleritis is a serious condition which needs prompt treatment
C   iritis presents with the redness mostly round the cornea
D   keratitis is particularly associated with rheumatoid arthritis
E   acute glaucoma may be intensely painful

26.2 In retinal vein occlusion

A   glaucoma is an important risk factor
B   the onset of symptoms usually occurs within minutes
C   there are characteristic haemorrhages in the affected sector of the
    retina
D   subsequent improvement in vision is rare
E   aspirin is indicated for long-term prophylaxis

**26.3 Diabetes is a risk factor for the development of the following
conditions:**

A   cataract
B   uveitis
C   glaucoma
D   retinal vein occlusion
E   episcleritis

SECTION 27: PSYCHIATRY

27.1 **The following statements about psychiatric disorders in mental patients are true:**

A   about 5% of medical inpatients have detectable psychiatric disorders

B   psychiatric co-morbidity prolongs patient stay in hospital

C   most medical patients with suspected depression should be referred to a psychiatrist

D   anxiety is a common cause of somatization

E   hypochondriacal complaints may be the first evidence of severe mental illness

27.2 **The following are true about anorexia nervosa:**

A   bingeing is rare

B   it may present with amenorrhoea

C   female patients lose pubic and axillary hair because of raised cortisol levels

D   the prognosis is improved by high calorie feeding via naso-gastric tube

E   untreated, about 1 in 4 patients die of their disease

27.3 **An 18-year-old man has recently become socially withdrawn and is reported to be behaving strangely**

A   the most likely diagnosis is schizophrenia

B   he should be admitted to a psychiatric hospital under a section of the *Mental Health Act*

C   at interview, he admits that he has been hearing his thoughts spoken out loud; this is a diagnostic symptom of schizophrenia

D   first rank symptoms at the onset of schizophrenic illness indicate a worse prognosis

E   after a first episode of schizophrenia about 50% develop a chronic disorder

27.4   The following are true about bulimia nervosa (BN):

A   BN typically has a later age of onset than anorexia nervosa
B   fluoxetine is useful in reducing the frequency of bingeing and purging
C   group cognitive behaviour therapy is contraindicated
D   1–2% of young women in Britain and North America fulfil the criteria for bulimia nervosa, the majority of whom have not come to medical attention
E   BN is associated with drug and alcohol abuse

27.5   The following are true about depression in elderly people:

A   the prognosis is worse than in younger patients
B   elderly people require lower doses of antidepressants to achieve a therapeutic effect
C   cognitive impairment is often detected on the Mini-Mental State examination
D   irritability is a common symptom compared with younger patients
E   electroconvulsive therapy (ECT) should not be given if the patient's depression is understandable

27.6   A 65-year-old woman presents to Casualty. She is unkempt and disorientated in time, place and person. She is admitted to the ward. The following are true:

A   she is noted to have a disturbed sleep pattern which makes the diagnosis of an acute confusional state more likely than one of a dementing illness
B   a past psychiatric history of schizophrenia makes a diagnosis of dementia more likely
C   one in 20 people over 65 years have Alzheimer's disease
D   aggressive outbursts make the diagnosis of delirium more likely than a dementing illness
E   the onset of delirium tremens is usually about 24 hours after the last alcoholic drink

27.7 **A 45-year-old patient who has taken an overdose of 50 paracetamol tablets is seen in casualty but refuses treatment. The following are true:**

A   he can only be compelled to receive medical treatment once he has been assessed by a psychiatrist

B   paracetamol and salicylates account for about 50% of reported overdoses

C   deliberate self-harm (DSH) is most common in people from social classes 4 and 5

D   DSH is associated with personality disorder in at least 25% of cases

E   chronic disabling diseases do not appear to increase the chance of later suicide

27.8 **The following are true about tricyclic antidepressants:**

A   they should be discontinued 3 months after recovery from a first depressive episode

B   they are rarely suitable for outpatients with suicidal ideation

C   are rarely used for the treatment of depression in patients over 80 years of age

D   are less effective than clonazepam in the treatment of anxiety disorders

E   should not be used if there is a history of ischaemic heart disease

SECTION 28: ALCOHOL AND DRUGS

28.1 The following facts about alcohol misuse are true:

A   the most useful marker of changes in alcohol consumption is serum gamma-glutamyl transpeptidase levels

B   alcoholic coma has a mortality rate over 30%

C   withdrawal symptoms occur most frequently 12–36 hours after abstinence

D   Wernicke's disease is due to folic acid deficiency

E   the peripheral neuropathy of alcohol abuse affects the upper limbs and cranial nerves more than the lower limbs

28.2 The following complications are recognized consequences of the abuse of the following substances:

A   hyperthermia and ecstasy

B   cardiac arrhythmias and glue

C   pulmonary oedema and cocaine

D   cardiac arrhythmias and heroin

E   candida infection and heroin

28.3 The symptoms of alcohol withdrawal include

A   atrial fibrillation

B   auditory hallucinations

C   jaundice

D   grand mal fits

E   hyperacusis

SECTION 29: FORENSIC MEDICINE

29.1 **Patients who have died in the following circumstances should be reported to the coroner:**

A   where the patient died within a year of an operation
B   where the patient may have died from an occupational disease
C   where the cause of death is unknown
D   where the patient was not seen immediately after death
E   where the cause of death is AIDS

29.2 **Brain stem death can be diagnosed when the following criteria are met:**

A   no respiratory movements when the patient is disconnected from the ventilator and the arterial PCO_2 has been shown to be less than 50 mmHg
B   absent corneal reflexes
C   absent gag reflex after tracheal stimulation
D   absent spinal reflexes
E   absent motor responses in cranial nerves

SECTION 30: SPORTS MEDICINE

30.1 **The following facts about exercise electrocardiography are true:**

A   exercise ECGs are the most useful test of coronary disease in asymptomatic middle-aged men at particular risk of coronary disease

B   asymptomatic men with abnormal ECGs are 10–20 times more likely to develop coronary heart disease than the general population

C   over half of asymptomatic men with abnormal exercise ECGs will have arteriographically normal coronary arteries

D   exercise ECGs should be avoided in men with angina because of the risk of myocardial infarction

E   exercise ECGs should be recommended regularly for middle-aged sportsmen

30.2 **In stress fractures**

A   X-rays may appear normal

B   a physiotherapist's ultrasound applicator can be a useful diagnostic test

C   bone scintography is the most accurate diagnostic test

D   the fourth and fifth metatarsals are the most commonly affected bones in the foot

E   rest for up to four weeks in a plaster of Paris cast is usually necessary

30.3 **The following statements about carbohydrate metabolism are true:**

A   the liver usually stores more glycogen than muscle

B   sugar or glucose consumption just before endurance exercise is to be recommended

C   fluids containing high glucose concentrations stimulate gastric emptying and therefore absorption

D   during the second half of a marathon the runner depends on fat rather than glycogen for fuel

E   adrenaline inhibits insulin secretion

SECTION 31: MEDICINE IN OLD AGE

31.1 **The following age-associated physiological changes occur in people aged over 65:**

A   a lengthening of clotting times indicating a tendency to bleeding following minimal trauma

B   a fall in haemoglobin concentration

C   an increase in the elasticity of the aorta and main branches accompanied by a decrease in their diameter and length

D   a fall in cardiac output at rest

E   a rise in residual lung volume

31.2 **The following facts about therapy in elderly people are true:**

A   about 10% of admissions to hospitals in the UK are drug-related

B   drug absorption is, in general, reduced

C   renal tubular secretion of penicillin is increased

D   the effect of warfarin on synthesis of clotting factors is decreased

E   potassium supplements should accompany thiazide diuretic therapy

31.3 **The following statements about heart disease in elderly patients are true:**

A   cardiac pain is usually more severe than in middle-aged patients

B   basal lung crepitations are diagnostic of heart failure

C   a third heart sound is more suggestive of heart failure than is a fourth heart sound

D   digitalis therapy is contraindicated in most patients because of the danger of toxicity

E   angiotensin-converting enzyme (ACE) inhibitors are of considerable value in the treatment of heart failure

SECTION 32: TERMINAL CARE

32.1 **The following statements about the care of patients with terminal illness are true:**

A   hyperalimentation increases survival in patients with advanced cancer

B   corticosteroids usually lead to an improvement in appetite

C   most chronic cancer pain is neuropathic

D   over three-quarters of patients with a painful bony metastasis gain significant relief from a single treatment with radiotherapy

E   haloperidol is usually effective in treating uraemic vomiting

32.2 **The following statements about the use of analgesics for terminal care are true:**

A   morphine is poorly absorbed when given by mouth

B   morphine passes through the blood–brain barrier quickly

C   diamorphine is superior to morphine in the treatment of severe pain

D   the plasma half-life of morphine is about 12 hours

E   epidural morphine is contraindicated because it may cause neuropathic leg pain

ANSWERS AND REFERENCES

Brackets have been used to indicate the answers which are false. The page references given next to each answer option refer to the Third Edition of the *Oxford Textbook of Medicine*. For example, 5.1 (A) 153 indicates that in our Section 5, question 1, the answer A is incorrect and that a further explanation of this item can be found in the *Oxford Textbook of Medicine* on page 153.

SECTION 5: IMMUNE MECHANISMS IN HEALTH AND DISEASE

5.1   **(A) 153**   **(B) 153**   C 153   **(D) 153**   E 153

Mast cells originate from bone marrow precursors and are mainly found in tissues, particularly in mucous membranes and connective tissue. Interferon, rather than mast cells, activates killer cells. Mast cells are intimately involved in the anaphylactic reaction via chemicals such as histamine and leukotriene (slow-reacting substance of anaphylaxis) which are found in their cytoplasm.

5.2   **(A) 158**   B 158   **(C) 158**   D 158   E 158

There are three specific histamine receptors. H_1-receptors have many functions and the new non-sedating H_1 antihistamine drugs, such as terfenadine and cetirizine, are important for controlling manifestations of allergic reactions. Ligation of H_2-receptors results in enhanced gastric acid and mucus secretion and bronchodilatation. H_3-receptor ligation induces the release of histamine and neurotransmitters but no H_3-antihistaminic drugs are available yet.

5.3   **(A) 159**   **(B) 159**   C 159   **(D) 159**   **(E) 159**

Flushing is commonly associated with anaphylaxis as are tachycardia and arrhythmias. Hypotension commonly occurs, often accompanied by bronchoconstriction.

5.4   A 160   **(B) 160**   **(C) 160**   D 160   E 160

Allergic rhinitis affects about 10% of European populations and is usually either seasonal due to pollens or perennial due to house-dust mite antigens or animal salivary protein antigens. Allergic rhinitis usually occurs before the fourth decade and decreases thereafter. IgE-mediated degranulation of mast cells and basophils stimulates the reaction, and it is the presence of IgE which forms the basis of the skin-prick testing and raised serum IgE levels diagnostic of the condition.

5.5   A   162   (B)   162   (C)   162   D   162   E   162

Desensitization involves the subcutaneous injection of ever increasing doses of soluble allergen extract up to a maximally tolerated maintenance dose in order to induce specific tolerance. Desensitization may safely be used in combination with pharmacological intervention.

5.6   (A)   162   B   162   (C)   162   D   162   (E)   162

Desensitization is not suitable for asthmatic patients in whom it may precipitate severe attacks. Many of the pollen and house-dust mite allergen extracts cause troublesome local reactions, occasionally anaphylaxis and even death and have not been demonstrated to be unequivocally efficacious.

5.7   (A)   166   (B)   166   C   166   (D)   166   (E)   166

Common varied immunodeficiency (CVID) presents at any age, but particularly in early childhood and late adolescence. Serum IgM levels may be normal or even raised. The prognosis for a patient with CVID varies according to the presentation but is rarely as poor as a five-year life expectancy. The cause of most cases is probably viral although the aetiological mechanisms remain obscure. Patients with CVID are not particularly prone to fungal infections.

5.8   A   175   (B)   175   (C)   175   D   175   E   175

Opsonization is probably the most important function of complement and involves the removal of the soluble immune complexes formed as a result of antibody/antigen interaction. The importance of complement lysis can be shown by the susceptibility to bacterial infections of patients with deficiencies of final lytic pathway components.

SECTION 6: CLINICAL ONCOLOGY

6.1   A   197   B   197   C   197   (D)   197   (E)   197

The pattern of rapidly increasing incidence of skin cancer with age is due to exposure to ultra-violet light. This pattern of rapidly increasing incidence of cancer with age probably reflects the cumulative effect of processes that operate throughout life. Nephroblastoma occurs only in childhood. Hodgkin's disease first appears in childhood and then continues to occur more or less evenly throughout life.

6.2 **(A) 198   B 198   C 198   D 198   (E) 198**
Cancer used to be more frequent in women than in men because of the great frequency, 70 years ago, of cervical carcinoma. Now cancer is more common in men. This fact, however, hides a huge variety of sex ratios of cancers of different organs as well as other cancers, with a great variation of incidence dependent on age, and environment. Oesophageal cancer shows great sex variation ranging from an equal distribution between the sexes to a 20-fold greater incidence among men.

6.3 **A 199   (B) 199   C 199   (D) 199   E 199**
Japan has a high incidence of stomach cancer, but a low incidence of ovarian, bladder and prostatic cancer. England has a high incidence of lung cancer and a low incidence of liver and nasopharyngeal cancer. The USA has a high incidence of prostatic, corpus uteri and colonic cancer. The high fibre diet prevalent in Nigeria probably protects against colonic cancer. The variation in the incidence of cancer is not confined to common cancers. It may be shown by many others. For example Burkitt's lymphoma never affects more than 1 in 1000 of any population, but is at least 100 times more common in parts of Uganda than it is in Europe.

6.4 **(A) 202   (B) 202   C 202   D 202   E 202**
Cancer of the nasopharynx occurs only marginally more commonly in men than in women. No convincing evidence has emerged of a strong genetic predisposition, although a weakly significant HLA type in Singapore has been reported. Nasopharyngeal cancer occurs very commonly in Southern China and may be linked to the 'salted fish' (better described as decomposing fish) on which children are commonly weaned.

6.5 **A 202   (B) 202   C 202   D 202   (E) 202**
All types of smoking have comparable effects on oesophageal cancer, as do all types of alcoholic drinks. Alcohol and tobacco act synergistically. The epidemiological features of oesophageal cancer are very different in Africa and Asia. The high incidence in Iran has been linked to extreme poverty, a restricted diet of home-made bread and tea, sheep's milk and very little fruit, vegetables or meat. In China during the 1970s oesophageal cancer was the second most common cause of death among cancers. However, large falls in this incidence are being reported, for reasons that are not fully understood. Oesophageal cancer has been linked with molybdenum deficiency in the soil and malnutrition.

6.6 **A** 210 **(B)** 210 **C** 210 **D** 210 **(E)** 210
Cervical cancer has always been rare in Jewesses and has tended to occur less commonly in Muslim women than in women of other faiths living in the same country (e.g. Hindu women in India). Squamous carcinoma make up the vast majority of cases. Cervical cancer is linked with the human papillovirus.

6.7 **(A)** 212 **(B)** 212 **(C)** 212 **(D)** 212 **(E)** 212
Neither the chronic irritation of bladder stones nor that of recurrent urinary tract infections appears to be linked with bladder cancer. Chlornaphthazine and cyclophosphamide are the two medicines linked with bladder cancer.

6.8 **(A)** 216 **B** 216 **(C)** 216 **D** 216 **(E)** 216
Phenacetin is linked with renal pelvic cancer and cyclophosphamide with bladder cancer. Combined oral contraceptives have been linked with both hepatoma and breast cancer (but not vaginal cancer) and have also been shown to decrease the risk of endometrial and possibly ovarian cancer.

6.9 **(A)** 217 **(B)** 217 **C** 217 **D** 217 **E** 217
Overall, occupational hazards are estimated to account for about 2–3% of all fatal cancers in developed countries. Radiologists are linked with marrow (not bone) cancer. Farmers and seamen are both prone to skin cancers because of their exposure to ionizing radiation.

6.10 **A** 218 **(B)** 218 **C** 218 **D** 218 **E** 218
Overnutrition may lead to an increase in the risk of breast cancer by bringing forward menarche and by increasing the formation of oestrogen from androstenedione in adipose tissue (when it becomes significant due to the absence of ovarian oestrogen). This formation of oestrogen from androstenedione is also the reason obesity may increase the risks of endometrial cancer. The increased excretion of bile salts characteristic of obesity may also increase the risk of cancer of the gall-bladder.

6.11 **(A)** 219 **B** 219 **C** 219 **(D)** 219 **(E)** 219
The preservation of food by salt appears to increase the risk of gastric cancer. A number of vitamins have been said to be protective against cancer: vitamin C reduces the risk of gastric cancer and vitamins A and E have also been said to have some protective effect, but there is no evidence to link vitamin D with a protective effect. Fibre protects against colonic cancer.

6.12 **(A) 227** **(B) 227** **(C) 227** **D 227** **E 227**
Epstein–Barr virus is linked with Burkitt's lymphoma and nasopharyngeal cancer. Papillomavirus is linked with cervical cancer.

6.13 **A 237** **(B) 237** **C 237** **D 237** **(E) 237**
CT should be used for detecting pulmonary metastases. It is capable of identifying metastases greater than 2 mm in diameter. Skeletal X-rays are very insensitive to the presence of bony metastases; skeletal scintigraphy is the method of choice. Ultrasound is a poor technique for detecting abdominal and pelvic lymphadenopathy because interference from bowel gas makes it difficult to examine all abdominopelvic nodal sites.

6.14 **(A) 243** **(B) 243** **C 243** **(D) 243** **E 243**
Stomach cancer is not an accepted cause of malignant hypercalcaemia. Thymoma is more likely to cause peripheral neuropathy, red cell aplasia and autoimmune disease than malignant hypercalcaemia. Most squamous cell tumours (including lung) can cause hypercalcaemia. Hodgkin's disease does not cause hypercalcaemia, but it does cause other paraneoplastic syndromes, such as seborrhoeic keratosis, thrombocytosis and dementia secondary to limbic encephalitis.

6.15 **A 249** **B 249** **(C) 249** **(D) 249** **E 249**
Combination chemotherapy depends for its efficacy on using agents that are known to be different (for example agents that cross-link DNA combined with drugs that are antimetabolites). Toxicity is the main limitation on treatment, so it is essential to combine agents with differing, or non-additive, toxicity.

6.16 **(A) 250** **B 250** **C 250** **D 250** **(E) 250**
Symptoms of carcinomatous meningitis usually develop over a few weeks and may be subtle at first. Focal fits are uncommon, and neck stiffness (unlike viral or bacterial meningitis) is not one of the more common features of the illness.

6.17 **A 250** **(B) 250** **C 250** **D 250** **(E) 250**
Cerebral metastases are ten times as common as primary brain tumours; they cause symptoms in 15% of all cancer patients during life. Metastases

are usually intradural of which 80% are found in the cerebrum and the rest in the cerebellum and elsewhere. Radiation is the most useful non-surgical treatment.

6.18 **A 255** **(B) 255** **C 255** **(D) 255** **(E) 255**
The usual radiation used for therapy is X-rays from a linear accelerator. However, tissues close to the skin surface can be treated with X-rays from a similar but lower energy apparatus. Brachytherapy is the delivery of radiotherapy by placing radioactive sources close to the tumour. Neutron irradiation is little used these days because recent data suggests there is no advantage over other modalities. Gamma-rays are generated from isotopes, such as cobalt-60, and electron beams are useful for radiotherapy where therapy needs to finish at a defined edge because there is a sharp reduction of dose beyond a certain depth, the depth being defined by electron energy.

6.19 **(A) 256** **B 256** **(C) 256** **(D) 256** **E 256**
The side-effects of radiotherapy are usually divided into acute and those appearing 6 months after the therapy (late). Cystitis appears 3–4 weeks after radiation. Cataract is a common late side-effect.

SECTION 7: INFECTION

7.1 **(A) 270** **(B) 270** **(C) 270** **(D) 270** **E 270**
Bartonella bacilliformis causes Oroya fever. *Chlamydia trachomatis* causes urethritis, conjunctivitis and salpingitis. *Brucella* sp. causes brucellosis, septicaemia, local infections, arthritis and meningitis.

7.2 **(A) 281** **B 281** **C 281** **D 281** **E 281**
Why so many infections are milder in childhood than adulthood has never been explained satisfactorily. It may be that immunopathological reactions are more marked in adults due to maturation of their immune system or because of previous exposure to cross-reacting antigen, but there are likely to be other explanations. Schistosomiasis is seen more frequently in young boys than in adults, probably because of the gradual acquisition of protective immunity by the adult, but also because boys bathe in rivers more frequently.

7.3 **A 293** **(B) 293** **C 293** **(D) 293** **E 293**
Fever potentiates the immune and inflammatory response. Fever is due to

the resetting of the anterior hypothalamic thermostat which in turn is due to the synthesis of prostaglandins in the brain. Fever can occur in the absence of infectious organisms when the temperature regulating centre (or pathways) is damaged by a neurological disease, such as stroke.

7.4 (A) 293   B 293   (C) 293   D 293   (E) 293
The earliest change in septic shock is peripheral vasodilation, although most of the increased flow appears to occur in arteriovenous anastomoses with stagnation in true capillaries. A pulmonary toxin has not been identified, but there is some evidence that a circulating myocardial toxin appears depressing myocardial function and causing left ventricular failure. Serum pH falls in septic shock, partly due to the accumulation of lactic acid because of glycolysis in anoxic tissues.

7.5 A 300   B 300   (C) 300   (D) 300   E 300
After oral administration the amount of drug absorbed is described as its bioavailability. It varies quite significantly amongst commonly prescribed drugs. Ampicillin has a bioavailability of 50%. Amoxycillin has a bioavailability of over 80%, much higher than ampicillin. Erythromycin is poorly absorbed and has a bioavailibility of 18.45%.

7.6 A 305   B 305   C 305   D 305   (E) 305
A patient with a history of penicillin sensitivity should avoid all beta-lactam drugs which include cephalosporins, carbapenums and monobactams. If a beta-lactam is essential, then it should only be used with full resuscitation equipment at hand.

7.7 (A) 306   B 306   C 306   D 306   (E) 306
All antimicrobials have some dose-related adverse effects. Fortunately, apart from a few exceptions, such effects are limited from a clinical point of view. The exceptions include aminoglycosides, amphotericin, quinine and zidovudine. For other antimicrobials, such as beta-lactams, the most common side-effects are idiosyncratic.

7.8 (A) 323   B 323   C 323   D 323   (E) 323
Yellow fever is the only vaccine for which there is still an international requirement before entry to some countries. Yellow fever is endemic only in tropical Africa and South America. Cholera vaccine is no longer

recommended by the WHO because it has significant side-effects and its efficacy is low. The standard meningococcal meningitis vaccine is not effective in developed countries because it does not protect against type B meningococcus, the most common cause of meningitis in those countries.

7.9 **(A) 324**   **B 324**   **(C) 325**   **(D) 325**   **(E) 325**

The most common causative agent of travellers' diarrhoea is *Escherichia coli*. Heating water to 100° Centigrade is necessary to kill most pathogens. Water filters retain a useful function and are widely recommended in developing countries. Short courses of empirical antimicrobials, for example ciprofloxacin, can be useful for travellers' diarrhoea, particularly for patients with underlying disease.

7.10 **(A) 325**   **B 325**   **(C) 325**   **D 325**   **E 325**

Commercial airlines will normally carry a woman up to 36 weeks of pregnancy. Live vaccines should be avoided in pregnancy. If there is a significant risk of yellow fever the vaccine should be administered because there is no recognized associated teratogenicity. Tetanus immunization is safe.

7.11 **(A) 335**   **B 335**   **C 335**   **D 335**   **E 335**

Rhinoviruses, unlike enteroviruses, are destroyed by acid and so do not cause gastroenteritis. The most common rhinovirus infection is the common cold, but rhinoviruses have also been detected in the middle ear fluid of children with acute otitis media and in sinuses during acute sinusitis.

7.12 **A 339**   **(B) 339**   **C 339**   **(D) 339**   **(E) 339**

RSV has a peak incidence at 2–6 months and most children (90–95%) have been infected by the age of two years. RSV has an incubation period of 2–8 days (mean 5 days) in healthy hosts. These hosts shed virus for up to 10 days, although this period can extend to 3–4 weeks in immunocompromised children. Ribavirin should not be used routinely for previously healthy children but it should be considered for children with immunological deficiencies or cardiopulmonary disease.

7.13 **A 339**   **(B) 339**   **(C) 339**   **D 339**   **E 339**

Influenza vaccines usually contain both influenza strains A and B. They are recommended for all elderly people, particularly those in a residential setting where the epidemic nature of influenza is particularly devastating. Vaccination of normal healthy children is not routinely recommended because the quality of natural immunity is superior to that from vaccination.

7.14   A   344   (B)   344   (C)   344   (D)   344   E   344
Ocular herpes may present with constitutional symptoms like fever. Preauricular lymphadenopathy is a well recognized sign in ocular herpes. Corneal scarring is not the expected outcome from ocular herpes, although the cornea and underlying stroma may be affected which can lead to corneal ulceration and scarring. Corticosteroids should be avoided as they can exacerbate symptoms and make the corneal damage more serious.

7.15   (A)   347   (B)   347   C   347   D   347   (E)   347
Humans are the only reservoir of chickenpox infection. Recurrent chickenpox is extremely rare. Chickenpox may cause encephalitis, the patient usually presenting with cerebellar signs or encephalopathy, but it is less serious than herpes simplex encephalitis and only has a mortality of about 5%.

7.16   (A)   354   (B)   354   C   354   (D)   353   (E)   353
Infectious mononucleosis (IM) is most easily and cheaply diagnosed by use of the Monospot test for heterophile antibodies in the patient's serum. IM is almost always more severe in adolescents and adults than in children, possibly because the former are capable of a more exuberant immunological reaction to the foreign body. Aspirin and bedrest are the recommended treatment for most uncomplicated adolescent cases. IM spreads characteristically sporadically. The IM fever may rise to 40°C during the day and marked swings are unusual.

7.17   A   355   B   355   (C)   355   D   355   E   355
Two types of lymphoma are being seen with increasing frequency in AIDS patients: large-cell lymphoma and Burkitt lymphoma. Both of these are associated with Epstein-Barr virus (EBV). EBV may play some part in the induction of Hodgkin's disease (HD) because of the similar socioepidemiology of HD with infectious mononucleosis (which is caused by EBV) and the fact that within 5 years of infectious mononucleosis there is a four to six-fold increased chance of developing HD. The association of EBV with nasopharyngeal carcinoma is so consistent that it is widely accepted that the virus has a role as a necessary agent, not sufficient on its own, in the causation of the cancer.

7.18   (A) **361**   (B) **361**   C **361**   D **361**   E **361**
Only 5% of all congenitally infected infants have typical cytomegalic inclusion disease, another 5% have atypical involvement. With cytomegalic inclusion disease, mortality may reach 20% and the outlook for normal development is poor. More than 90% of symptomatic patients develop central nervous and sensory defects later in life.

7.19   A **369**   (B) **369**   (C) **370**   D **371**   (E) **371**
Human orf is an occupational hazard for farmers, shepherds, sheep handlers and vets. Person-to-person transmission is unusual. In most cases the patient remains well and generalized disease is very rare. Most patients require no specific treatment. Anti-microbials to prevent secondary infection may be indicated. Topical idoxuridine in dimethylsulphoxide has been used in some cases.

7.20   (A) **372**   (B) **372**   C **372**   (D) **372**   (E) **374**
Mumps has an incubation period of 14–18 days. A patient excretes virus in the saliva for two to six days before symptoms develop and virus can be detected in urine for up to 14 days around the onset of the illness. Mumps is transmitted by close personal contact with a patient who is excreting the virus in the saliva. There is no immunological or virological evidence for a link between mumps and diabetes. Abortion may occur in women with mumps in the first three months of pregnancy but it is not common.

7.21   (A) **375**   (B) **375**   (C) **375**   (D) **375**   E **375**
MMR vaccine uses live, attenuated viruses. A single vaccination at 12 months gives lifelong immunity, although some countries, such as the USA and Sweden, recommend a second dose, given at either 5 or 12 years.

7.22   A **379**   B **379**   (C) **375**   (D) **375**   (E) **375**
Measles subclinical infection is rare. Pneumonia is the most common complication of measles to cause death. Fever, leucocytosis and respiratory difficulties are the early symptoms. Bronchopneumonia is the most common form and is usually caused by *S. aureus*. Lobar pneumonia may be caused by *Strep. pneumoniae*. Following an attack of measles lifelong immunity is almost invariable. Since 1987 when two million children globally were estimated to have been killed by measles, annual mortality has dropped to the current figure of about 900,000 cases each year.

7.23 (A) **390**   (B) **393**   C **393**   D **393**   (E) **394**
Viruses are well established as a cause of food poisoning, possibly accounting for nearly one-half of cases in infants and young children. The only virus to be identified in vomitus is Norwalk agent. Injected human pooled gammaglobulin is not used to prevent food poisoning; there has been a trial of oral gammaglobulin which showed it could protect from disease associated with rotavirus in endemically affected nurseries but could not prevent babies from becoming infected.

7.24 A **397**   B **397**   C **397**   (D) **397**   (E) **397**
Rabies virus cannot penetrate intact skin although it can penetrate intact mucosa. Transmission from one person to another has been reported in four patients who received corneal grafts. Rabies virus can replicate locally in muscle cells or attach to the motor or sensory nerve endings.

7.25 (A) **409**   B **409**   C **409**   (D) **409**   (E) **409**
The characteristic pink, maculopapular rash of rubella usually starts on the face and spreads to the trunk and finally the extremities. Mouth ulcers appear in many conditions but not particularly rubella. Orchitis is characteristic of mumps.

7.26 (A) **411**   (B) **411**   C **411**   D **412**   (E) **412**
It is generally accepted that naturally acquired immunity to rubella lasts longer than the immunity of vaccination. Vaccination is not offered to pregnant women who have been exposed to rubella because of the concern that the vaccine virus might be teratogenic, however studies show that the maximum theoretical risk is less than 5%. Vaccinees cannot infect other people although the infection can cross the placenta.

7.27 A **418**   (B) **418**   (C) **418**   D **418**   (E) **418**
The initial phase of yellow fever (the period of infection) is characterized by headache, fever, lumbosacral pain, nausea and prostration. On examination the patient is feverish, with a relative bradycardia, conjunctival injection and a coated tongue reddened along the edges. The patient may recover within days (the period of remission) only to relapse again (the period of intoxication) with much more serious symptoms and signs. The patient often complains of generalized myalgia, but not peripheral neuropathy.

7.28 **(A) 419**   **(B) 419**   **(C) 419**   **D 420**   **E 422**
Although *Ae. aegypti* is the main mosquito vector, there are other vectors, *Ae.albopictus, Ae. polynesiensis*, and several species of *Ae. sculettaris* species. In the last 10 years the incidence of dengue haemorrhagic fever (DHF) has risen sharply. Many more children than adults are affected by DHF. The management of DHF is entirely symptomatic the purpose being to correct hypovolaemia. Monitoring the haematocrit is valuable because a sharp rise will indicate significant plasma loss and early volume replacement may prevent shock. Prognosis depends on early detection.

7.29 **A 430**   **B 430**   **(C) 430**   **(D) 432**   **E 434**
It has been estimated that more than 100,000 infections with Lassa fever occur each year, with several thousand deaths. Lassa fever causes an acute deafness in one or both ears in about one-third of affected patients. About half these patients show a complete recovery 3–4 months after onset, but the other half continue with significant sensorineural deafness.

7.30 **A 440**   **B 440**   **C 440**   **(D) 440**   **(E) 442**
Ebola virus is classified as a haemorrhagic viral fever. Many patients develop the bleeding, usually five to seven days after onset of symptoms. The gastrointestinal tract and lungs are most frequently involved. Laboratory investigation shows profound haemostatic dysfunction. Ebola virus is not particularly nephrotoxic but is destructive to many organs including the liver and spleen. Therapy is limited to nursing care and supportive measures. No vaccine is yet available and ribavirin is ineffective.

7.31 **A 467**   **(B) 474**   **C 474**   **D 474**   **E 476**
P. carinii remains the most common life-threatening opportunistic infection in those who progress from chronic HIV infection to AIDS. The presentation of tuberculosis is subacute with malaise, fatigue, weight loss and shortness of breath. Miliary tuberculosis occurs in AIDS but, surprisingly, is rare. Cerebral toxoplasmosis usually results from reactivation of toxoplasma cysts in the brain leading to abscess formation. About 5–10% of people with CD4 counts below 50/µl develop cytomegalovirus retinitis which usually presents with visual loss, blurring of vision or scotoma.

7.32 **(A) 481**   **B 481**   **(C) 482**   **D 481**   **E 481**
There is no good clinical evidence that zidovudine alters the rate of

seroconversion following accidental parenteral exposure to HIV-infected blood. That said, many units offer the therapy, taking the empirical view that possible benefits outweigh possible disadvantages. The Concorde trial showed that asymptomatic patients need not be treated immediately following seroconversion. About one-third of AIDS patients treated with zidovudine develop anaemia which is dose dependent and reversible if the drug is stopped. Overall, the incidence of zidovudine side-effects increases with HIV disease progression.

7.33   A   483   (B)   484   C   484   (D)   487   E   485
The course of AIDS in developing countries does appear different from that in industrialized countries where most seropositive adults are asymptomatic for several years and die with an AIDS-defining illness. Women are infected earlier than men, possibly because of their earlier sexual debut and rapid changes of partner in some communities. Staphylococcal infection is not particularly associated with AIDS, but *Strep. pneumoniae* infection is and bacterial pneumonia is a common sign of underlying HIV infection.

7.34   (A)   494   (B)   493   C   493   (D)   494   (E)   495
A negative Schick test indicates that the person has previously been exposed to diphtheria and the resulting immunity makes them less likely to develop the illness. Diphtheria is caused by *Corynebacterium diphtheriae*. Diphtheria does spread by lymphatics but it does not cause severe local necrosis or damage. A potentially fatal complication of diphtheria is paralysis of the larynx and pharynx but this is invariably temporary if the patient can be kept alive during the acute phase.

7.35   A   498   B   498   C   498   D   498   E   498
Streptococcal vulvovaginitis is often secondary to an infection elsewhere, for example the throat. Streptococcal perianal disease is a superficial, well-demarcated rash which spreads out from the anus in association with itching, rectal pain and blood-stained stools. In many cases of erysipelas there is good evidence of *S. pyogenes*, but other streptococci may also cause the condition.

7.36   (A)   503   B   503   C   503   D   503   E   503
The streptococcal infection that precipitates rheumatic fever must occur in the throat, for reasons that are not fully understood. Other unknowns include

why some families are more susceptible than others and why some serotypes of *S. pyogenes* are more toxic and common than others. Detection of raised antibody levels or changes in sequential samples is often the only reliable evidence of recent streptococcal infection because the organism may be isolated from as few as one in four patients by the time the disease has appeared. Since patients who have had rheumatic carditis are at greater risk of the disease recurring (possibly without a symptomatic sore throat) there are some physicians who would recommend antimicrobial prophylaxis well into adulthood and possibly for life.

7.37   A 504   (B) 504   (C) 504   D 504   E 504
The arthritis of rheumatic fever affects large joints characteristically, like knees and hips. It is usually not symmetrical. The painful joint swelling characteristic of the complication is reduced within 24 hours of the administration of salicylates. There is some evidence that it may be less common in tropical countries, although this may simply be due to later admission to hospital in poorer, tropical countries. The differential diagnosis of rheumatic arthritis includes infective arthritis, drug reactions and serum sickness.

7.38   A 520   (B) 520   (C) 520   (D) 521   (E) 521
Penicillin penetrates poorly into the CSF so high doses must be maintained throughout the course of pneumococcal meningitis. Vancomycin is very expensive and quite beyond budgets. The role of dexamethasone in the treatment of pneumococcal meningitis remains uncertain but there is no evidence its administration causes increased abscess formation. Penicillin does not precipitate sickle cell crises.

7.39   A 524   B 524   (C) 525   D 525   (E) 525
S. aureus is permanently carried in the nose by about 25% of the population, and about the same number do not carry the organism at all. The remaining 50% carry the organism intermittently. Most strains of *S. aureus* produce beta-lactamase, but a few do not. Erythromycin resistance is found in about 5% of patients, although this proportion can reach 20% in patients with skin disease.

7.40   (A) 547   B 547   C 547   D 547   (E) 549
Epididymo-orchitis is an uncommon complication of urethral gonorrhoea,

occurring in less than 2% of cases. Resistance of the gonococcus to cephalosporins is rare, for example therapeutic failure with ceftrioxone is undocumented.

7.41   **(A)** 552   **(B)** 552   C 552   **(D)** 552   E 552
Salmonella infection is not readily transmitted from person to person except in people living in closed communities, in old people and infants. Provided a *Salmonella*-excreting food handler does not have diarrhoea and is healthy, there is no reason to suspend him or her automatically from work. Some patients with *Salmonella* poisoning vomit but frequent vomiting is rarely a feature.

7.42   A 553   B 554   C 554   **(D)** 554   **(E)** 554
Shigellosis is the most communicable of all bacterial infections, needing only a small infective dose (as few as 10–100 bacteria can cause dysentery), and is generally transmitted from person to person by the faecal-oral route. Co-trimoxazole and ampicillin have, for many years, been the antibiotics of choice for shigellosis, but most strains are now resistant. Resistance to ciprofloxacin is currently uncommon, apart from *Sh. dysenteriae*.

7.43   A 558   B 558   **(C)** 558   D 558   **(E)** 558
The infectivity of campylobacters is low, partly because they withstand drying very poorly. Campylobacters are the most common 'cause' of Guillain-Barré syndrome, the incidence in studies ranging from 14% to 38%. Erythromycin remains the drug of first choice in the treatment of campylobacter enteritis; in most countries resistance rates have remained as low as 5%.

7.44   A 560   B 560   C 560   D 560   E 560
Many organisms produce toxins which may be either endotoxins or exotoxins. However it is not always clear what the precise role of the toxins on the gut is. For example, *Shigella dysenteriae* produces a powerful exotoxin (Shiga toxin) which is associated with the haemolytic uraemic syndrome but what other part in the disease process it plays is unclear.

7.45   A 562   B 562   **(C)** 562   D 562   E 562
The fever of typhoid rarely starts abruptly, rigors are uncommon and, when fully developed, the fever reaches a plateau of 39–40°C. Constipation is

characteristic early in typhoid followed by diarrhoea. Hypertension may occur in typhoid and is a serious prognostic development.

7.46   **A**   **577**   **(B)**   **578**   **(C)**   **579**   **D**   **579**   **(E)**   **580**
Man is the only known mammalian host and natural victim of *V. cholerae*. Cholera usually starts with painless, watery diarrhoea. In children complications are both more frequent and severe. They include stupor, coma, convulsions, pulmonary oedema and cardiac arrhythmias. Immunization has not proved effective in altering the transmission of cholera or the convalescent carriage of *V. cholerae*.

7.47   **(A)**   **587**   **B**   **588**   **(C)**   **588**   **(D)**   **588**   **E**   **589**
Bordetella pertussis is very much a bacterium. Atectasis occurs as a consequence of bronchial obstruction by the thick mucus characteristic of whooping cough, but bronchiectasis is rare. Passive immunization with immunoglobulin has no place in the treatment of whooping cough. Pertussis vaccines are not usually given after the age of 6 because of the likelihood of local reactions.

7.48   **A**   **595**   **B**   **595**   **(C)**   **596**   **D**   **596**   **(E)**   **598**
Buboes are very painful lymphatic swellings which most commonly appear in the groin, axilla or neck depending on where the patient was bitten by the infecting flea. The antibiotic of first choice in the treatment of the plague is still intramuscular streptomycin. Tetracycline is a good alternative, and for patients with meningism, chloramphenicol.

7.49   **A**   **608**   **(B)**   **608**   **C**   **608**   **D**   **609**   **(E)**   **610**
Yersiniosis appears worldwide and in some countries contributes about 1–3% of all cases of enteritis. The onset may mimic acute appendicitis with pain in the middle or lower right quadrant of the abdomen, a fever and signs of peritoneal irritation. Pharyngitis, cellulitis, wound infections, pyomyositis, osteomyelitis, conjunctivitis, urinary tract infection, renal disease and pneumonia are some of the extraintestinal presentations of yersiniosis. Uncomplicated cases of yersiniosis should not be treated with antimicrobial therapy; in complicated cases third generation cephalosporins, quinolones or aminoglycosides are indicated.

7.50 **(A)** **619** **(B)** **619** **C** **619** **(D)** **619** **E** **620**

The worldwide incidence of brucellosis is rising although estimation is difficult because of lack of statistics and a notification system. In endemic areas inhalation of organisms is the most common mode of transmission. Others include ingestion of infected material, penetration of intact or abraded skin, conjunctival splashing, transplacental transmission, breastfeeding, unprotected sexual intercourse and blood transfusions. Brucellosis tends to affect children particularly in endemic areas because of their contact with farm animals.

7.51 **(A)** **624** **B** **624** **C** **625** **D** **627** **(E)** **627**

Under anaerobic conditions tetanus bacillus releases two toxins, of which only vanospasmin has clinical effects. It is transported retrogradely up peripheral nerves to reach the motor neurone cell bodies of the spinal cord and brainstem from where it reaches the sympathetic chain and parasympathetic centres. An attack of tetanus does not confer immunity and so the patient needs to be actively immunized after recovery.

7.52 **A** **628** **(B)** **628** **(C)** **628** **D** **628** **E** **628**

The intrathecal use of tetanus antiserum is best avoided because its efficacy remains unproven. Local infiltration of tetanus antitoxin is still practised in some units on the basis that it will neutralise any newly liberated or unbound tetanus toxin. For this reason it is important the antitoxin is introduced locally before the wound is surgically manipulated. Penicillin is the routine treatment of choice and more recently metronidazole has also been recommended.

7.53 **A** **648** **(B)** **651** **(C)** **652** **D** **646** **E** **646**

The overall mortality for all forms of tuberculosis in Great Britain is about 8%, varying from under 1% in children and adolescents to over 30% in those aged 75 years or more. Most patients with tuberculosis are well enough to be managed as outpatients following diagnosis. Concurrent HIV and *M. tuberculosis is* becomingly increasingly common and is the reason tuberculosis is fast re-emerging as a fatal disease in adults in developed countries. For this reason preventative chemotherapy in HIV patients is strongly recommended.

7.54 **A** 650 **(B)** 650 **C** 650 **D** 650 **E** 650
There are characteristic radiological appearances in patients with pulmonary tuberculosis, but it is also true tuberculosis may cause almost any radiological abnormality and atypical pictures are not uncommon. There is no particular reason why tuberculosis should cause right ventricular hypertrophy.

7.55 **(A)** 674 **B** 674 **C** 674 **D** 674 **(E)** 674
There is no simple, specific skin test (such as the Mantoux test in tuberculosis) for leprosy. The main source of infection in the community is nasal secretions from untreated or lapsed patients, but *M. leprae* is also secreted in the breast milk of untreated mothers. Although treatment with monotherapy can be effective, compliance rates and relapse rates have been much improved. When a high degree of cell-mediated immunity is developed, the infection remains localized.

7.56 **A** 690 **B** 690 **C** 690 **D** 690 **(E)** 690
About 60% of patients with Lyme disease will develop mono- or oligoarticular arthritis. Large or small joints may be equally affected. In about 10% of patients, involvement of large joints leads to erosion of cartilage and bone. From as early as 4 days to 3 months after onset of Lyme disease, about 10% of patients develop cardiac symptoms, such as atrioventricular block, cardiomegaly and acute myopericarditis. Ophthalmic complications are not a particular feature of Lyme disease.

7.57 **A** 700 **B** 700 **(C)** 700 **D** 700 **(E)** 700
Headache, myalgia, fever and chills occur in over 85% of cases of leptospirosis. Other common features include diarrhoea, arthralgia, cough, sore throat, bone pain, splenomegaly, lymphadenopathy and hepatomegaly.

7.58 **A** 703 **(B)** 703 **C** 703 **D** 704 **E** 704
Yaws is caused by *Trepomena pertenae*, a spirochaete that is morphologically identical to *Trepomena pallidum*, the cause of venereal and non-venereal syphilis. These trepomenes share common antigens so that infection by one species produces varying degrees of cross-immunity to the others. Bejel is found in semi-nomadic people of the Sahara desert regions. Improved standards of living, better medical care and mass penicillin treatment campaigns have reduced the prevalence. The lesion of yaws and other

treponematoses is largely due to the host's immune response rather than to toxic substances provided by the treponeme.

7.59   (A)   725   B   725   C   725   (D)   725   (E)   725
A wide variety of complications of Legionnaire's disease have been described, probably due to a multisystem toxic effect rather than from direct spread of the bacterium which appears to be rare. Acute respiratory failure occurs in up to 20% of cases. Acute, but reversible, renal failure occurs in severe disease.

7.60   A   745   B   745   (C)   746   (D)   746   E   746
Over 90% of cases of cat scratch fever have had contact with a cat, usually a young kitten. However, there have been occasional reports of injuries resulting from other animals or inanimate objects also resulting in cat scratch disease and the role of fleas in the transmission of cat scratch disease is still to be elucidated. The Frei skin test is used to diagnose lymphogranuloma venerum. Antimicrobials have not yet been shown to be generally effective in the treatment of cat scratch disease, although rifampicin, ciprofloxacin and gentamicin may benefit some patients.

7.61   (A)   751   (B)   751   (C)   751   (D)   751   E   751
There is no evidence that chlamydiae cause acute symptomatic prostatitis. However detection of chlamydiae in the chronic phase of prostatitis in a few patients may mean that a portion, at least, of chronic disease is due to chlamydiae. *C. trachomatis* is responsible primarily for epididymo-orchitis in developed countries; the organism has been found in at least one-third of epididymal aspirates in the USA and UK.

7.62   (A)   754   B   754   C   754   D   755   (E)   755
Psittacosis is caused by *C. psittaci,* is equally common in both sexes, is uncommon in children and mostly affects adults aged 30–60 years old. Psittacosis is rarely responsible for extrapulmonary complications but these include endocarditis, myocarditis, pericarditis, encephalitis, meningitis and hepatosplenomegaly. Pregnant women may suffer abortion if exposed to sheep suffering from enzootic abortion during the lambing season. Culture diagnostic techniques still have the greatest force in cases of litigation whereas serological results, for example, have limited value.

7.63 **(A) 801** **(B) 802** **C 803** **D 803** **E 803**
Mycetoma is a chronic infection involving subcutaneous tissue, bone and skin but without systemic effects. Pityriasis versicolor is a superficial infection which causes a very common (in the tropics) rash. Dermal penetration does not occur and nor does systemic involvement.

7.64 **A 831** **B 831** **C 831** **(D) 831** **E 831**
Metronidazole and tinidazole are the drugs of choice in the treatment of amoebiasis. A favourable response to medical treatment, even of amoebic abscess, occurs in about 85% of patients. Chloroquine continues to be a reserve drug in hepatic amoebiasis, but has little amoebicidal activity in the gut wall. Proguanil is a biguanide which is used as a prophylatic against sensitive strains of malaria. Erythromycin has amoebicidal action and is safe and useful in infants and young children.

7.65 **A 835** **(B) 835** **C 835** **(D) 835** **E 835**
The female *Anopheles* mosquito prefers to feed on blood in the evenings and night so that she can then rest while digesting the meal before flying off to lay eggs at a carefully selected water site. Since most *Anopheles* mosquitoes are selective in their breeding sites, it is possible that a knowledge of preferred sites can be helpful in control. *Anopheles* mosquitoes incline their bodies at an angle while feeding by contrast with other mosquitoes who hold their bodies parallel to the skin.

7.66 **(A) 846** **B 846** **C 846** **(D) 846** **(E) 854**
Patients with cerebral malaria may have mild meningism but neck rigidity and photophobia is rare, as is papilloedema. Unfortunately more than 10% of African children who survive cerebral malaria suffer sequelae such as hemiplegia, cortical blindness, epilepsy, ataxia and mental retardation. Dexamethasone has been shown to increase the length of coma and the incidence of gastrointestinal infection.

SECTION 8: CHEMICAL AND PHYSICAL INJURIES AND CLIMATIC AND OCCUPATIONAL DISEASES

8.1 **A 1048** **B 1048** **C 1048** **(D) 1048** **(E) 1048**
Antidotes exist for many drugs but they are seldom used. Their use in appropriate circumstances can be life-saving, but many are toxic in their

own right. Naloxone is used for opiate analgesics, methionine for paracetamol overdosage and flumazenil for benzodiazepines.

8.2 **A 1049**   **(B) 1049**   **(C) 1049**   **D 1049**   **(E) 1049**
Gastric lavage for self-poisoning is usually indicated only up to 1 hour after ingestion of the poison. Advice should always be sought, however, from a Poisons Centre because some drugs release their active ingredients slowly (e.g. theophylline), or require metabolic activation before becoming toxic (e.g. paracetamol). Clinically severe poisoning remains an indication for gastric lavage, even if the patient is unconscious. Clearly precautions must be taken to ensure gastric contents are not aspirated into the lungs. There is no evidence that gastric lavage prevents further episodes of self-poisoning. Contraindications to gastric lavage include ingestion of petroleum distillates since they rapidly cause pneumonitis and ingestion of corrosive poisons since lavage will increase the chances of perforation of the oesophagus or stomach.

8.3 **A 1058**   **(B) 1058**   **(C) 1058**   **(D) 1058**   **E 1059**
Tricyclic antidepressant overdosage continues to be a significant cause of mortality because these drugs are still the most widely used for the treatment of depression, and secondly because they are given to depressed people who are intrinsically more prone to self-poisoning. Tricyclic overdosage does not cause a rise in blood pressure but it may cause cardiac arrhythmias and tachycardia which can be difficult to treat. The natural inclination to use anti-arrhythmic drugs should be resisted because they can make matters worse. Attention to supportive measures such as adequate oxygenation and control of acidosis may be more rewarding. The great majority of patients poisoned with tricyclic antidepressants recover, even if they have ingested more than 250 mg although, clearly, the higher the dosage the greater the mortality. Charcoal haemoperfusion is ineffective, mainly because only a small proportion of the body load of tricyclics circulates in the vascular compartment.

8.4 **A 1080**   **B 1080**   **(C) 1080**   **D 1080**   **E 1080**
Hypoglycaemia may occur within 6–36 hours of ethanol overdosage due to inhibition of gluconeogenesis. The patient is often in coma and hypothermic, but other recognized features of hypoglycaemia such as flushing, sweating and tachycardia may be absent. Hypoglycaemia is

usually unresponsive to glucagon and so intravenous glucose is indicated. Blurred or double vision is a well recognized feature of severe ethanol intoxication, as is hypothermia. Depressed reflexes are more characteristic of ethanol poisoning than hyperreflexia.

8.5   **A 1167**   **B 1167**   **(C) 1167**   **(D) 1167**   **E 1167**
Occupational cancers are estimated to contribute 2–8% of cancers in an industrialized country like the US. Polynuclear aromatic hydrocarbons are produced in industries like iron and steel foundries, gas production, aluminium refineries and coke oven manufacture. Workers exposed to soot, pitch, tar and petroleum products are also at risk. The lung, skin and bladder are the sites of action of these compounds. Aromatic amines are known to be bladder carcinogens and are important in dyestuffs and antioxidants in dye production. They are also used in the rubber industry. For some occupations linked with cancers such as boot and shoe manufacture, furniture making and painting the specific carcinogen has not yet been identified.

8.6   **A 1168**   **(B) 1168**   **(C) 1168**   **D 1168**   **E 1168**
Repeated low impact trauma is thought to lead to the development of repetitive strain injury. The wrist and forearm are most commonly affected and shoulder and neck as well. Coal-face workers and dancers put repeated heavy impact loading on their bones and joints causing a quite different syndrome.

8.7   **(A) 1188**   **B 1188**   **C 1188**   **(D) 1188**   **E 1188**
Females and males are equally susceptible to acute mountain sickness. The faster the ascent, whether on foot, horseback, by train or air, the worse the acute mountain sickness. In particular, the more nights spent acclimatising *en route*, the less severe the mountain sickness is. If exertion is great (for example coping with snow or carrying heavy loads) acute mountain sickness is more likely.

SECTION 9: PRINCIPLES OF CLINICAL PHARMACOLOGY AND DRUG THERAPY

9.1   **(A) 1237**   **B 1237**   **C 1237**   **D 1237**   **E 1237**
The therapeutic index of a drug is the ratio of the dose at which unwanted effects become clinically important to that at which therapeutic benefit can

be expected. The therapeutic index is not calculated precisely because precise estimates of values would be impossible. However drugs are divided into two categories, those with high and low therapeutic indices. Thus penicillin has a high index because, in the absence of hypersensitivity, very large doses can be given safely. Aminoglycoside antibiotics have a low therapeutic index because the balance between the drug that brings benefit and toxicity is very fine.

9.2   **(A) 1242**   **B 1242**   **C 1242**   **(D) 1242**   **E 1242**
First pass metabolism is metabolism of a drug before it enters the systemic circulation. This does not only happen in the liver but may also occur in the gut lumen (for example insulin), the gut wall (for example isoprenaline) and the lungs (for example various amines). The absorption of propranolol, co-trimoxazole and cephalexia is increased in patients with coeliac disease. In migraine, reduced gastric motility reduces drug absorption, so metoclopramide can be helpful. Severe diarrhoea may result in enteric-coated formulations passing intact through the gut.

9.3   **A 1252**   **(B) 1252**   **C 1252**   **D 1252**   **(E) 1252**
In anaphylactic shock the drug interacts with IgE molecules fixed to cells, especially mast cells and basophil leucocytes, which triggers the release of the pharmacological mediators (histamine, 5-hydroxytryptamine, kinins) which causes the allergic response. The clinical signs include urticaria, rhinitis, bronchial asthma and angio-oedema.

SECTION 10: NUTRITION

10.1   **(A) 1282**   **B 1282**   **(C) 1282**   **D 1282**   **E 1282**
The word *kwashiorkor* comes from the Ga language of Ghana indicating the condition that a displaced (one who has been displaced from the mother's breast) child develops. It therefore typically affects children aged one to two years. Loss of muscle mass is not a typical feature – loss of muscle mass occurs in marasmus more typically. Hepatomegaly is frequently found. The liver is smooth, firm, painless and may extend to the iliac brim. The enlargement is due to fat, mainly triglyceride, accumulation.

10.2   **(A) 1286**   **B 1286**   **C 1286**   **(D) 1286**   **(E) 1286**
Marked changes in hormonal balance occur in malnutrition. Growth

hormone levels are usually raised in tandem with low insulin levels and a reduced insulin response to a test meal. There is, generally, glucose intolerance with glucose levels lower than normal. This is partly due to liver dysfunction because there is a similar extent of galactose intolerance and significantly reduced gluconeogenesis.

10.3   **(A)   1290**   **B   1290**   **C   1290**   **(D)   1290**   **E   1290**
In malnutrition there is reduction in gastric acid, bile and pancreatic enzyme production. The motility of the whole intestine is reduced so that transit time in the small intestine is increased. At the same time cellular enzymes and transport systems for the various components of food, for example carbohydrate, fat and protein, become damaged leading to loss of absorption. That this loss is one of capacity and not a specific abnormality can be shown by noting that if small amounts of food are presented, absorption is nearly normal. But if larger amounts are presented capacity is quickly overwhelmed.

10.4   **A   1296**   **(B)   1296**   **C   1296**   **(D)   1296**   **E   1296**
The three central features of anorexia nervosa (AN) are low birth weight, an intense and morbid fear of fatness and amenorrhoea. AN is largely confined to Western women aged 10–30 years, often from upper socio-economic groups. Less than 10% of cases are men. There is preservation of axillary and pubic hair in AN, unlike in patients with hypopituitarism.

10.5   **(A)   1300**   **B   1300**   **C   1300**   **(D)   1300**   **(E)   1300**
Most patients with bulimia nervosa (BN) can be managed as outpatients. Hospitalization is only required if there is severe depression, or a risk of suicide or if the patient's physical health is of concern, or if the patient is in the first trimester of pregnancy because of the increased risk of spontaneous abortion, or if outpatient care proves unsuccessful. Appetite suppressants have no beneficial effect in BN. Patients with BN do not appear to be more prone to other psychiatric disease.

10.6   **(A)   1302**   **B   1302**   **C   1302**   **(D)   1302**   **E   1302**
With increasing age a greater proportion of fat is distributed intraperitoneally. Surveys of height and weight in representative samples of men and women performed in the UK in 1980, 1987 and 1991 showed that the prevalence of obesity in both sexes increased between the ages of 16 and 50, and

continued to increase in women up to the age of 64. However, in men it declined after the age of 50. Obese people tend to be insulin-insensitive which is what makes them prone to diabetes.

10.7   **A** **1308**   **B** **1308**   **(C)** **1308**   **(D)** **1308**   **E** **1308**

Aromatase is the enzyme which converts androgens to oestrogens and in obese people there is more aromatase in adipose tissue than in the gonads which may account for the increased polycystic disease, infertility and menstrual problems encountered in obese people. Sex-hormone-sensitive cancers like prostate, breast and cervix occur more readily in obese people, but not stomach cancer. Obese people are prone to diabetes but not pancreatitis.

10.8   **(A)** **1318**   **(B)** **1318**   **C** **1318**   **D** **1318**   **E** **1318**

The recommended oral intakes of many trace elements are quite different from those for intravenous nutrition because the gut only absorbs a proportion (often as little as 10%) of these nutrients. Toxicity may thus develop if there is prolonged intravenous administration of trace elements at recommended oral levels. Patients in chronic liver failure have a high body sodium due to a secondary aldosteronism even though their serum sodium is low, often markedly low.

10.9   **A** **1321**   **B** **1321**   **C** **1321**   **D** **1321**   **E** **1321**

Nausea and/or vomiting is the most common complication of enteral feeding occurring in 10–20% of patients. Potassium disturbances are well recognized, depending on the patient's renal and gastrointestinal function as well as the potassium content of the feed. Five to 30 per cent of patients suffer from diarrhoea, the cause of which is not entirely understood. Antibiotic therapy, bacterial contamination of the feeds, the use of laxatives, and lack of dietary fibre may be contributory factors. Constipation may be a problem in long-term enteral nutrition, particularly in elderly, inactive patients.

10.10   **(A)** **1321**   **B** **1321**   **(C)** **1321**   **D** **1321**   **(E)** **1321**

Although Coca-Cola® contains significant quantities of caffeine, there is no evidence it affects intellectual function in patients with cerebral palsy. Blocked enteral nutrition tubes may well be unblocked by Coca-Cola®. Alternatives include water flushing followed by warm sodium bicarbonate solution or by digesting the coagulated feed with pancreatic enzymes. Coca-Cola® does not have a recognized role in stimulating lactation, but in underdeveloped countries it can be useful in rehydrating dehydrated children. Daily bathing with 10% formaldehyde solution of hands and feet affected by viral warts is recommended in preference to Coca-Cola® which has no known role in this respect.

SECTION 11: METABOLIC DISORDERS

11.1   **(A)**   **1338**   **B**   **1338**   **C**   **1338**   **D**   **1338**   **E**   **1338**
Early diagnosis of inborn errors of metabolism is essential to minimize the emotional trauma. The couple should then decide if abortion is necessary and acceptable to them. The cells obtained by amniocentesis are a valuable aid to pre-natal diagnosis but the procedure is performed at the fifteenth or sixteenth week of pregnancy.

11.2   **(A)**   **1343**   **(B)**   **1343**   **C**   **1343**   **D**   **1343**   **E**   **1343**
Ehlers–Danlos syndrome is a hereditary disorder of connective tissue which affects the arrangement of collagen fibres and leads to hyperelasticity of the skin (it is also known as cutis laxa) and of joints. Niemann-Pick disease is a lipoid storage disease in which abnormal sphingomyelin is deposited in reticulo-endothelial cells causing hepatosplenomegaly, mental deficiency, blindness, deafness and death usually before the age of 2 years.

11.3   **(A)**   **1376**   **B**   **1376**   **(C)**   **1376**   **D**   **1376**   **E**   **1376**
The prevalence of gout has increased in the Western world, for example by more than threefold in the past 10 years in the USA, where it is now the most common cause of inflammatory arthritis in men over the age of 40. Smoking and ACE inhibitor drugs are not recognized risk factors for gout. Chronic lead poisoning used to be a major risk factor for gout because of contamination of wine and other drinks by lead-containing glass bottles, or lead-glazed pottery or stoneware. In south-eastern USA soldered truck radiators are used for stills in the making of illicit moonshine alcohol, and these contaminate the alcohol with lead.

11.4   **A**   **1376**   **B**   **1376**   **C**   **1376**   **D**   **1376**   **(E)**   **1376**
Gouty arthritis occurs mainly in postpubertal men, and seldom in premenopausal women. Proteinuria is found in 20–30% of patients with

gout but the major renal insufficiency that occurs in most patients with gout is largely eye-related and does not reduce life expectancy. Hypertension occurs in 25–50% of patients with gout. Hypertriglyceridaemia occurs in over 75% of patients with gout; heavy alcohol intake and being overweight are additional predisposing factors. Gouty tophi are deposits of urate crystals deposited, for example, in periarticular fibrous tissue, or cartilage of the external ear.

11.5   A   1380   (B)   1350   C   1352   (D)   1356   (E)   1362
There are about 3000–4000 inherited diseases. The transmission of these can be via autosomal dominant, autosomal recessive, sex-linked recessive or sex-linked dominant traits. Autosomal recessive traits are the most common. Galactosaemia, cystinosis and phenylketonuria are all autosomal recessive.

11.6   (A)   1392   B   1392   (C)   1392   D   1392   (E)   1392
There are a great number of different factors which may precipitate attacks of acute porphyria in patients with the genetic trait. Great care must be taken to prevent exposure to them. Drugs are the most important and common precipitant. Other factors that may trigger an attack include alcohol ingestion, reduced calorie intake due to fasting or dieting and infection. Attacks are more common in females and rarely occur before puberty or after the menopause. Phenylalanine containing foods are problematic for people with phenylketonuria, but not for those with porphyria.

11.7   A   1397   B   1397   (C)   1397   (D)   1397   E   1397
Over 200 drugs have been classified as unsafe in acute porphyria because they have been shown to be porphyrinogenic in animals or *in vitro* systems, or to have been associated with acute attacks in humans. There are, however, about 200 drugs which are classified as being safe.

11.8   A   1406   (B)   1406   C   1406   (D)   1406   E   1407
Heterozygous familial hypercholesterolaemia (HFH) is dominantly inherited, affecting about 1 in 500 people in Britain and the USA. Raised serum cholesterol levels are characteristically found right through childhood. Tendon xanthomata appear from the age of 20, most commonly over the knuckles and in the Achilles tendons. HFH does not cause most affected people to become overweight and most do not have risk factors for coronary

heart disease other than hypercholesterolaemia. It does cause decreased catabolism of low density lipoprotein as a consequence of which this lipoprotein remains in the circulation for longer.

11.9 **(A) 1413**   **B 1413**   **(C) 1413**   **D 1413**   **E 1413**
Lipid-lowering therapy is not indicated automatically at some arbitrary serum cholesterol level in those patients in whom diet has failed. Many factors have to be taken into account and it is quite reasonable to avoid therapy in patients with serum cholesterol levels as high as 8 mmol/l provided no other significant coronary heart disease risk factors exist and particularly if cardioprotective high density lipoprotein cholesterol concentrations are high and contribute to the raised total cholesterol concentrations. Few patients with familial hypercholesterolaemia achieve significant reductions in serum cholesterol levels on diet alone.

11.10 **A 1416**   **B 1416**   **(C) 1418**   **(D) 1417**   **(E) 1416**
Maintenance of copper homoeostasis depends uniquely on its excretion in bile, with around 1.5 to 1.7 mg excreted daily. A much smaller amount is excreted in urine. Any interruption of the secretion of bile leads to accumulation in the liver followed by other organs. Wilson's disease is an autosomal recessive disorder characterized by abnormal accumulation of copper in the liver. Menke's disease is an X-linked disorder in which low circulating levels of copper and caeruloplasmin result in poor growth, mental retardation and abnormal 'steely hair'. Copper is an essential part of several key enzyme systems, for example lysyl oxidase, cytochrome oxidase and superoxide dismutase, but is not essential for neuromuscular function.

11.11 **(A) 1423**   **B 1423**   **(C) 1423**   **D 1423**   **(E) 1423**
Mental lethargy and emotional disorders are recognized features of zinc deficiency but not frank mental retardation. Zinc inhibits histamine release from mast cells and interferes in cell mediated immunity thus predisposing zinc deficient individuals to infection. Alopecia is characteristic of zinc deficiency rather than hirsutism, and diarrhoea tends to occur rather than constipation.

11.12 **A 1429**   **(B) 1429**   **C 1429**   **D 1429**   **(E) 1429**
Bone growth and mineralization are deficient in Gaucher's disease leading

to pathological fractures, bone infarcts and avascular necrosis of the femoral head. As well as grey-brown pigmentation of the forehead, hands and pretibial region, yellow-brown discolouration of subconjunctival areas in the region of the corneoscleral junction occurs. Anaemia is due to a combination of bone marrow replacement, hypersplenism and haemorrhage associated with thrombocytopenia.

11.13 **A 1448** **(B) 1448** **C 1448** **(D) 1448** **E 1448**
Both acute and chronic pancreatitis can cause diabetes mellitus as well as haemochromatosis. Albinism is due to a defect of the tyrosinase enzyme, and is not associated with diabetes. Endocrine conditions causing diabetes include Cushing's syndrome (excessive cortisol production), acromegaly (excessive growth hormone production), glucagonoma (excessive glucagon) and phaeochromocytoma (excessive adrenaline).

11.14 **(A) 1449** **(B) 1449** **(C) 1449** **D 1449** **(E) 1449**
Diabetes mellitus does not particularly affect collagen metabolism. Both macroangiopathy and microangiopathy are contributive causes to diabetic foot ulcers. An automatic neuropathy causing disordered small vessel blood flow (but not venous congestion) also contributes. Diabetes does not particularly damage the lymphatic system. A sensory, rather than motor, neuropathy is a further contributory cause.

11.15 **(A) 1450** **B 1450** **(C) 1450** **(D) 1450** **E 1450**
Type I diabetes appears to be caused by autoimmune destruction of the Islets of Langerhans, whereas type III diabetes seems to be the result of an initially exocrine pancreatic lesion caused by many small calculi in the distal branches of the pancreatic duct. Type I diabetes used to be known as juvenile onset diabetes and can rarely be managed without insulin because of the degree of islet cell destruction. The aetiology of type II diabetes is still largely hereditary but it may also be linked to foetal nutrition, specifically placental deficiencies. Type III diabetes rarely occurs beyond the tropics, including those born in the tropics who later leave. It is particularly common in India and East Africa.

11.16 **(A) 1459** **B 1459** **(C) 1459** **(D) 1459** **E 1459**
The vagal nerve rather than the sympathetic nerve is responsible for stimulating insulin release. Glucagon promotes insulin secretion and in turn insulin promotes glucagon secretion. The stimulatory acetylcholine and the inhibitory dopamine probably both act at the cytoplasmic calcium level to

achieve their effects. An important inhibitory agent is somatostatin which is secreted by the D cells of the Islets of Langerhans.

11.17 A 1467 (B) 1467 C 1467 D 1467 (E) 1467
Food intake in diabetics should be spread evenly throughout the day, aiming for three main meals and at least three snacks. Foods with a high fibre content (especially the viscous type) are encouraged because they slow digestion and absorption and thus even out the peaks and troughs of plasma glucose levels. Diabetes should aim at a ratio of polyunsaturated to mono-unsaturated to saturated fatty acids of about 2:2:3.

11.18 (A) 1469 (B) 1469 C 1470 (D) 1471 (E) 1471
The mechanism of action of sulphonureas is not wholly clear. In part they stimulate insulin secretion from beta cells in the pancreas. The hypoglycaemic effectiveness of sulphonylureas often decreases with time. About 30% of diabetics on these drugs will be transferred to insulin within four years. Sulphonylureas are relatively contraindicated in young, thin type I patients, particularly if they are ketotic. There is no recognized benefit from combining sulphonylureas with biguanides.

11.19 A 1473 (B) 1473 C 1473 (D) 1473 (E) 1473
Human insulin differs from porcine insulin at one amino acid site in the B-chain. It differs from bovine insulin at two further sites. Human insulin is slightly less antigenic than both bovine and porcine insulin but the more important factors in antigenicity are purity of preparation and change of injection sites. Human insulin is more quickly absorbed from injection sites than porcine insulin, which in turn is more quickly absorbed than bovine insulin. It is not particularly prone to causing fat atrophy. So far no convincing evidence has emerged to show human insulin is more effective than porcine insulin: they appear to have comparable potency.

11.20 (A) 1474 B 1474 C 1474 (D) 1474 (E)? 1474
Shallow subcutaneous injections are absorbed more rapidly than deeper ones. Intradermal injections are more slowly absorbed while intramuscular ones are more quickly absorbed. Massage, hot baths and exercise will speed absorption. Insulin absorption is quicker from the abdomen than from the arm or thigh.

11.21 (A) 1482 (B) 1482 C 1482 (D) 1482 E 1482
There has been an improvement in mortality as well as morbidity in diabetic

patients. Older data indicated the average expectation of life, for example, of a type I patient diagnosed before the age of 30 to be a further 29 years. Recent data has seen that life expectation extended to 35 years. The overall mortality rate for type I patients is about five times that of the general population, but over 60% can still expect to reach the age of 50. Diabetic nephropathy is the second most common cause of death in diabetic patients after cardiac causes.

11.22 A 1485   B 1484   (C) 1484   (D) 1484   E 1484
Retinopathy is more common in type I patients but, overall, about 4% of diabetic patients have clinically observable retinopathy at diagnosis, and some 15% have changes on retinal photography. Although retinopathy occurs in most patients, a significant minority (about 10–15% of type I diabetics) can be diabetic for 40 or 50 years without evidence of retinopathy.

11.23 A 1514   B 1514   (C) 1514   (D) 1514   E 1514
The second most common presentation of amyloid A protein amyloidosis is organomegaly, specifically thyroid enlargement and hepatosplenomegaly. The heart is affected in 90% of cases of immunoglobin light chain amyloidosis, with restrictive cardiomyopathy and right ventricular failure being the most common presentations. Arrhythmias due to involvement of the conducting system are also common. Skin involvement in amyloidosis does not cause dermatomyositis but may cause the appearance of papules, nodules and plaques usually on the face and upper trunk. Involvement of blood vessels commonly results in purpura occurring either spontaneously or after minimal trauma.

11.24 A 1536   (B) 1536   C 1536   D 1536   E 1536
The sum of the measured plasma cations is normally greater than the sum of the cations by about 14 mmol/l. The difference is known as the anion gap and is largely due to negatively charged proteins but also to phosphate, sulphate and some organic acids. The anion gap is used in diagnosing the various types of metabolic acidosis and in following the progress of therapy. Causes of a metabolic acidosis with a normal anion gap include the causes of direct loss of bicarbonate from the body, either through the gut (for example diarrhoea or through pancreatic fistulae or ureterosigmoidostomies), or through the kidney (for example renal tubular acidosis or acetazolamide therapy).

SECTION 12: ENDOCRINE DISORDERS

12.1   **(A)** 1575   **B** 1575   **C** 1575   **(D)** 1576   **(E)** 1576
ACTH is secreted by the pituitary gland and stimulates the adrenal cortex
to secrete cortisol, adrenal androgens and mineralo-corticoids. ACTH is
secreted in bursts, these bursts increasing in frequency after 3–5 hours of
sleep and reaching a maximum in the hours just before awakening and for
about one hour after awakening. The bursts reduce in frequency thereafter.
In Addison's disease and Nelson's syndrome circulating levels of ACTH are
extremely high, causing the pigmentation of skin found in these conditions.

12.2   **(A)** 1584   **(B)** 1584   **C** 1582   **(D)** 1582   **(E)** 1582
Random serum growth hormone (GH) estimation is not a particularly
useful test of GH deficiency because GH is secreted in a pulsatile fashion
so values in a normal person may vary greatly within 24 hours. To
diagnose GH deficiency effectively a stimulation test (such as the
insulin stress test) is needed. GH does not appear to be required for
growth *in utero* so deficiency causes no complications in this respect.
GH deficiency occurs in obesity. Hypersecretion of GH is found in
anorexia nervosa, hepatic failure and type I diabetes.

12.3   **A** 1588   **B** 1588   **C** 1588   **(D)** 1588   **E** 1588
Sudden visual compromise is usually caused by sudden expansion of a
pituitary tumour due to serious haemorrhage into it. Children with Cushing's
disease who have not responded to pituitary irradiation are in need of
surgical treatment. Surgery within the cavernous sinuses is too dangerous.
Tumours there must be treated with drugs or radiotherapy or both. In some
patients with prolactinoma medical treatment with bromocriptine fails and
surgical treatment is indicated.

12.4   **A** 1592   **(B)** 1592   **C** 1592   **D** 1592   **(E)** 1592
The dermatological features of acromegaly include acne, greasy skin, skin
tags and hyperhidrosis due to hypertrophy of the sebaceous and sweat
glands. Spinal mobility is normal or increased but backache is common,
particularly when dorsal kyphosis is present. Disc spaces are increased and
paraspinal ligaments become hypertrophied and lax. Galactorrhoea is
common in female acromegalics, but rare in men. It may be due to the
hyperprolactinaemia which occurs in 40% of acromegalics, but in the

absence of hyperprolactinoemia is idiopathic or the result of the iatrogenic effect of growth hormone. A prevalence of 38% of acromegalics suffering from obstructive sleep apnoea has been reported, particularly in men. Cardiovascular disease is the most common cause of death in acromegalics. Myocardial hypertrophy, interstitial fibrosis of the myocardium and lymphomononuclear carditis are all common findings at autopsy. Valve complications are not a feature.

12.5 **(A) 1604** **(B) 1605** **(C) 1605** **D 1606** **E 1606**
The thyroid is unique among endocrine glands in that it stores much preformed hormone. Less than 1% of both T3 and T4 circulates free in the plasma. The main (about 75%) protein which binds T3 and T4 is thyroxine-binding globulin. Thyroglobulin is the main precursor of thyroid hormones. T4 is secreted from the thyroid gland and is partly converted in the plasma into T3 as a consequence of enzymatic monodeiodination.

12.6 **(A) 1644** **(B) 1643** **(C) 1643** **D 1644** **E 1643**
In children with Cushing's syndrome growth arrest is almost invariable and is due to glucocorticoid excess. The characteristic myopathy involves the proximal muscles of lower limb and shoulder girdle. Thinning of scalp hair is common, often accompanied by hirsutism. Bruising of the skin with little or no trauma is an important sign.

12.7 **(A) 1644** **(B) 1644** **C 1646** **D 1645** **(E) 1647**
Very few laboratories have developed methods for the measurement of free levels of plasma cortisol. In normal subjects plasma cortisol levels are at their highest first thing in the morning and reach a nadir at around midnight. In those with Cushing's syndrome the morning plasma cortisol level is normal and it is the nocturnal level which is raised. Serum potassium concentrations are normal or low in Cushing's syndrome, especially in ectopic ACTH syndrome when low serum potassium is particularly common.

SECTION 13: PREGNANCY

13.1 **A 1723** **B 1723** **C 1723** **(D) 1723** **(E) 1723**
Combined oral contraceptives suppress some menstrual disorders, particularly menorrhagia and dysmenorrhoea. As a consequence, complications such as hospital admissions for dilation and curettage and for hysterectomy,

and for iron deficiency anaemia are reduced. There is a significant (up to 50%) reduction in the need for surgical biopsies for benign breast disease in long-term users of the pill. The risk of epithelial ovarian cancer (and endometrial cancer) is reduced by up to 50% in women who have used the pill for at least 2–3 years. Longer use provides added protection, and the benefit appears to persist for many years after cessation of smoking. Epidemiological studies appear to show no association between breast cancer and the pill, although some recent UK studies show that prolonged early use of the pill may increase the risk of breast cancer. Most research has indicated an association between long-term oral contraceptives and cervical cancer, but this finding cannot yet be regarded as established.

13.2   **A**   **1731**   **(B)**   **1731**   **(C)**   **1731**   **D**   **1731**   **E**   **1731**

All drugs should be avoided if possible during pregnancy. The benefits for mother or foetus of treating mild-to-moderate hypertension are far from clear-cut, in particular there is good evidence that the treatment of moderate long-term hypertension does not prevent superimposed pre-eclampsia. If treatment is necessary, methyldopa is a popular choice because its use during pregnancy has been so closely researched, and its safety established by case control studies. Long-term beta-adrenergic blockade is not recommended throughout the second and third trimesters because its use has been linked with significant foetal growth retardation. ACE inhibitors are contraindicated in the second and third trimesters because there is evidence they cause foetal and neonatal renal impairment. Clonidine and prazosin may be used safely during pregnancy but would not be popular choices.

13.3   **A**   **1735**   **(B)**   **1735**   **C**   **1735**   **(D)**   **1735**   **(E)**   **1735**

Peripheral vasodilation is a common finding in pregnancy, probably mediated by gestational hormones. Vasodilation, increased heat production and the low resistance uteroplacental circulation are three significant causes of the low blood pressure commonly found in pregnancy. During pregnancy the stroke volume increases contributing (with an increased heart rate) to a rise in cardiac output. There is a fall in tidal lung volume and an increase in respiratory rate which often causes breathlessness which can easily be misdiagnosed as heart failure. A diastolic murmur in pregnancy is not physiological (unlike a soft systolic murmur) and should be investigated further. The anaemia sometimes found in pregnancy is not due to a fall in red cell mass.

SECTION 14: GASTROENTEROLOGY

14.1   **A**   1821   **B**   1822   **(C)**   1822   **D**   1822   **E**   1822

Morning vomiting occurs in pregnant women, alcoholics and those with metabolic disorders such as uraemia. Psychological disorders can cause vomiting during or soon after a meal. Vomiting immediately after a meal is particularly associated with pyloric canal ulcers. Delayed vomiting may be caused by peptic ulcer, gastric carcinoma, gall bladder disease and intestinal obstruction. Projectile vomiting is associated with pyloric stenosis and raised intracranial pressure.

14.2   **A**   1822   **B**   1822   **(C)**   1822   **(D)**   1822   **E**   1822

Referred pain is due to the sharing of central pathways by peripheral neurones, for example back and leg pain is associated with intestinal distension. Colonic pain is often poorly localized but frequently radiates into the thighs or back. Ninety per cent of the nerve fibres in the vagus are sensory but none of them transmit pain. Pancreatic pain is often helped by curling up and usually made worse by lying flat. Small-intestinal pain is central and midline, usually colicky, and radiating into the back.

14.3   **A**   1826   **(B)**   1826   **(C)**   1826   **D**   1826   **E**   1826

The definition of what constitutes constipation is difficult. In western Europe three-quarters of the population pass about one stool per day, weighing about 200 g. However, there are many normal individuals who pass only two to three stools a week or alternatively two to three a day. Most clinicians consider a change in bowel habit by the individual as the significant evidence to focus on. Hyperthyroidism causes diarrhoea rather than constipation, but hypothyroidism is a commonly missed cause of intractable constipation. Hypercalcaemia, rather than hypocalcaemia, causes constipation. Constipation occurs almost invariably in Parkinson's disease for reasons not fully understood, but it is probably part of the disease process rather than simply a consequence of immobility.

14.4   **(A)**   1827   **B**   1827   **(C)**   1827   **(D)**   1827   **(E)**   1828

Rather than being avoided, clinicians should be more inclined to put central lines into older patients because of their vulnerability to circulatory collapse. In most adults transfusion of 1 unit of blood should raise the haemoglobin by 1g/dl. The routine use of nasogastric tubes is probably not indicated. They are uncomfortable, they may cause fresh bleeding or even erosions which may be confusing at subsequent endoscopy. Monitoring the pulse rate is a more effective means of detecting rebleeding. Trials with H_2-antagonists (and with proton pump inhibitors) have shown that reducing gastric acid secretion is not generally indicated in the acute management of gastrointestinal bleeding.

14.5 **(A) 1846**   **(B) 1846**   **C 1846**   **D 1846**   **E 1847**
The prevalence of dental caries is greatest in children and young adults although an increasing number of root caries are occurring later in life. Functionally and quantitatively the most important sugar is sucrose which gives rise to heavy plaque formation. Caries occurs when sugars are converted by enzymes to lactic and other organic acids causing the pH inside the plaque to fall to the critical 5.5 level. The destructive process works slowly through the enamel layer but once dentine is reached it accelerates quickly. There is no overwhelming evidence to support the use of fluoridated toothpaste for adults, but the fluoride does make a difference for children.

14.6 **A 1853**   **(B) 1853**   **(C) 1853**   **(D) 1853**   **(E) 1855**
Recurrent oral ulcers are the most common lesions affecting the mouth, the prevalence varying between 10–34%. Their aetiology has not been established but there is no evidence vitamin deficiency (or food allergy) is involved. Some families appear more prone to recurrent oral ulcers, as are younger populations aged 10–40. Oral ulcers may extend to vulvovaginal sites but this development is part of Behcet's syndrome.

14.7 **(A) 1861**   **(B) 1861**   **(C) 1861**   **D 1861**   **E 1861**
Radiotherapy, rather than chemotherapy, commonly causes xerostomia which usually stops several months after treatment has finished. Drugs which may cause xerostomia include antihistamines, phenothiazine, diuretics and atropine. Other diseases, rather than affecting the salivary glands directly, may cause xerostomia by affecting fluid balance of which diabetes, anaemia and dehydration are common examples.

14.8 **(A) 1867**   **(B) 1867**   **C 1867**   **D 1867**   **(E) 1868**
Stopping smoking, losing weight and raising the bedhead have all been traditional remedies routinely recommended but recently their value has

been re-evaluated. Avoidance of large meals and provocant food and drinks and physical activities are measures worth trying. Currently proton-pump inhibitors do appear to be the treatment of choice for oesophagitis and reflux. There is no good evidence, yet, that long term acid suppression is linked to oesophageal or gastric carcinoma. However, extensive follow-up is still being done.

14.9 **(A) 1869** **(B) 1869** **(C) 1869** **D 1869** **(E) 1869**
Oesophageal manometry is the only sensitive method for demonstrating achalasia; in the absence of dilatation barium meals are often reported as normal. Cramping chest pain may accompany the dysphagia so achalasia is not a painless condition. Difficulty swallowing solids invariably occurs more commonly than swallowing fluids. Increasing oesophageal regurgitation may cause aspiration and respiratory symptoms thereby. Drugs are generally ineffective for achalasia and surgery remains the best option.

14.10 **(A) 1874** **B 1874** **C 1874** **D 1874** **(E) 1874**
Medications can damage oesophageal mucosa because it is susceptible to injury through pH-dependent and other mechanisms. Pills pass relatively slowly through the normal oesophagus so that complications such as poor pill design or pill taking technique can quickly lead to oesophageal damage. Slow-release potassium chloride, tetracycline, non-steroidal anti-inflammatory agents and quinidine are medications at highest risk of causing severe injury. Captopril and slow-release theophylline may also cause damage.

14.11 **A 1877** **(B) 1877** **C 1878** **(D) 1878** **E 1878**
It is now recognized that the strongest aetiological factor for duodenal ulcer is infection of the gastroduodenal mucosa with *H. pylori*. Not only does eradication of the *H. pylori* lead to healing of the duodenal ulcer, but it also causes a dramatic reduction in the incidence of ulcer relapse. *H. pylori* is also associated with other gastrointestinal diseases including chronic gastritis, gastric ulceration and gastric cancer. Duodenal ulcers do not occur in anacidic patients, just as they almost invariably occur in the presence of gross hypersecretion of acid as in the Zollinger-Ellison syndrome. Patients with duodenal ulcers on average secrete more acid than healthy controls and have also been found to have more parietal cells.

14.12 A 1881   (B) 1881   (C) 1881   (D) 1881   E 1881
The diagnosis of the Zollinger-Ellison (Z-E) syndrome initially depends on the detection of an elevated plasma gastrin concentration in the presence of acid in the stomach. Gastrin is measured by radio-immunoassay using antibodies with varying affinity to the different molecular species of gastrin. The islet-cell tumour of the Z-E syndrome is often small and difficult to identify. The secretin test is the most reliable confirmatory investigation. Injection of secretin in normal people causes a fall in plasma gastrin but in those with the Z-E syndrome there is an immediate rise. The H_2-antagonists have now been replaced as the medication of choice by the proton-pump blocker omeprazole. Most patients will respond to 40 mg b.d. of omeprazole.

14.13 A 1892   B 1892   (C) 1892   D 1892   E 1877
Gastrin release is particularly stimulated by protein ingestion and gastric distension. Its main action is the stimulation of gastric acid secretion, primarily from parietal cells. Patients with duodenal ulcer appear to have *H. pylori*-induced hypergastrinaemia. They also have an exaggerated gastrin response to food and continue to secrete gastrin despite high acid levels in the antrum.

14.14 (A) 1897   (B) 1897   C 1897   D 1897   E 1897
The characteristic feature of the carcinoid syndrome is the flush. It usually affects the head and upper chest and is associated with tachycardia, hypotension and increased skin temperature. Occasionally patients experience a sensation of great heat and wheezing may occur. Rarely other symptoms such as increased lacrimation and facial oedema occur. Precipitating factors include alcohol, food ingestion, emotion, stress or exertion but most attacks are unprecipitated. The secretory diarrhoea is profuse with passage of several litres a day (instead of the normal 150–200 ml a day), and sometimes nausea, vomiting or abdominal pain. Cardiac valve abnormalities are almost invariably right-sided, affecting about 50% of patients. They result from endocardial fibrosis.

14.15 (A) 1916   B 1916   (C) 1916   (D) 1919   E 1920
Coeliac disease is an inflammatory disease affecting the small intestine caused, in most individuals, by gluten in the diet. The characteristic, but not specific, histological feature is loss of villous height. The mucosal thickness is usually normal or minimally reduced because the crypts become elon-

gated, usually known as crypt hypertrophy. The best test to diagnose coeliac disease is intestinal biopsy. This used to be done by biopsy of the duodenal-jejunal junction by use of a Crosby capsule, but recently distal duodenal biopsies taken at endoscopy have been found to be successful. The two significant complications of coeliac disease are ulcerative jejunoileitis and T-cell lymphoma.

14.16 **(A) 1924   B 1924   C 1924   D 1924   (E) 1924**

Pigmentation rather than vitiligo is a feature of Whipple's disease, usually in advanced disease. The arthritis may affect up to 90% of patients and is migratory, non-deforming, affecting peripheral joints and seronegative. It often precedes gut involvement by several years. Respiratory complaints include pleurisy and pulmonary infiltrates. Hypotension, rather than hypertension, may occur.

14.17 **(A) 1932   (B) 1933   (C) 1933   (D) 1934   E 1933**

Tropical sprue predominantly occurs in southern and south-east Asia, the Caribbean islands and, to a lesser extent, Central and South America. It virtually never occurs in Africa. Unlike most diarrhoeal diseases, tropical sprue affects adults more than children. The illness usually starts with an attack of acute diarrhoea, fever and malaise following which, after a variable period, the patient settles into the chronic phase of diarrhoea, steatorrhoea, weight loss, anorexia, malaise and nutritional deficiencies. The aetiology of tropical sprue is unknown. Histological and physiological changes due to tropical sprue occur in the stomach, small bowel and colon.

14.18 **(A) 1937   (B) 1937   (C) 1937   D 1938   E 1939**

Crohn's disease affects young adults but all classes equally. There are not any marked sex differences. Smokers have a 4–6 times greater risk of developing Crohn's disease than non-smokers, in contrast to ulcerative colitis which is negatively associated with smoking. Crohn's disease occurs in both partners of marriages very rarely which makes it unlikely that environmental factors alone are responsible for the disease. Isolated cases of the mouth, oesophagus, stomach and anus are recognized, but they are rare – generally the whole of the gastrointestinal tract is involved histologically. Amyloid is a well recognized complication which can affect either the bowel or systemic sites such as the liver, spleen and kidney.

14.19 **A** **1941** **(B)** **1941** **C** **1941** **(D)** **1941** **E** **1938**
An abdominal mass is much more likely to be due to Crohn's disease (CD) than ulcerative colitis (UC), particularly if small-intestinal disease is present. In CD thickened bowel can also often be palpated. Bloody diarrhoea would almost certainly be due to UC. Pneumaturia would occur as a consequence of fistula formation into the urinary system and is therefore more common in CD. Other urinary system complications include involvement of the ureters (usually the right) leading to sterile pyuria, urinary tract infection or hydronephrosis. The rectal mucosa in CD is often normal, but almost always inflamed in UC.

14.20 **(A)** **1943** **(B)** **1944** **C** **1945** **(D)** **1948** **E** **1951**
Ulcerative colitis (UC) occurs worldwide although eastern Europe, Asia, Japan and South America appear to have a low incidence. UC is not becoming more common, in contrast to Crohn's disease. UC usually presents with a gradual onset of symptoms such as diarrhoea, rectal bleeding, and the passage of mucus. Most patients will then develop an individual pattern of intermittent attacks interspersed with periods of remission. Only 10–15% of patients have a continuous chronic course with negligible periods of remission. Only a few (5%) have a severe first attack and then no more attacks. Corticosteroids should be reserved for acute attacks because they lose effectiveness with long term use and because of their side-effects. Women with UC have normal fertility, are not at increased risk of abortion, and pregnancy does not appear to be a risk factor for relapse.

14.21 **(A)** **1952** **B** **1953** **C** **1953** **D** **1955** **(E)** **1955**
The gastrointestinal tract is composed of three muscle layers: the muscularis mucosa just beneath the mucosa, the circular layer, and finally the longitudinal layer whose fibres run parallel to the gut lumen. Gut innervation is intrinsic made up of two major plexuses, Auerbach's plexus and Meissner's plexus; and it is extrinsic made up of sympathetic and parasympathetic nerves. The parasympathetic supply is predominantly by the vagus nerve whose fibres are 80% sensory. During sleep the colon exhibits minimal motor activity unlike the stomach and small bowel which show marked periodicity.

14.22 **(A)** **1961** **B** **1961** **C** **1961** **D** **1961** **(E)** **1961**
Postoperative ileus occurs as a consequence of motor paralysis of the

gastrointestinal tract due to neural dysfunction. The colon is inert after surgery but activity returns rapidly to the stomach. This gastric activity, though, may be ineffective. Biliary gastritis may occur when the ability of the pylorus to work as a sphincter is damaged by surgery. The gastritis may be due to the detergent action of the bile acids on gastric mucosa. Non-obstructive gastric stasis occurs after vagotomy but it rarely lasts long as there is considerable functional adaptation after vagotomy.

14.23 **(A) 1966** **(B) 1966** **(C) 1966** **D 1966** **E 1966**
Inflammation of the rectal and sigmoid mucosa would rule out irritable bowel syndrome (IBS) as a diagnosis. These findings would be much more characteristic of ulcerative colitis or Crohn's disease. Abdominal palpation may elicit pain but, not usually, colonic thickening. A sigmoid colon containing faeces is often palpable. There are no specific radiological, endoscopic or haematological findings which can confirm the diagnosis of IBS. The passage of mucus in the faeces is compatible with IBS, but faecal blood makes this diagnosis most unlikely.

14.24 **(A) 1969** **B 1969** **C 1969** **D 1970** **(E) 1970**
Basal intracolonic pressures are similar in healthy people and those with diverticular disease. The difference occurs when the colon is stimulated by food, drugs or emotion. In those with diverticular disease high pressures are generated in affected colonic segments. Diabetic patients are prone to diverticular disease at an earlier age than normal. The striking feature of a fully developed diverticulum is the muscle atrophy which leaves it without any muscular layer and therefore, of course, vulnerable to perforation. Diverticular disease both shortens the colon and significantly narrows the lumen.

14.25 **(A) 1981** **B 1981** **C 1981** **(D) 1981** **(E) 1981**
Although finger clubbing can occur with almost any malignancy, oesophageal carcinoma is not one with which this sign is characteristically associated. Hoarseness is a well recognized feature and indicates involvement of the recurrent laryngeal nerve. Metastases, most commonly to regional lymph nodes, occur in about 50% of patients at diagnosis. The earliest spread is locally but subsequently occurs to gastric glands and then to the liver. Palpable cervical lymph nodes are often the only physical signs found apart from weight loss. The dysphagia of oesophageal carcinoma is

unrelenting and progressive, unlike the dysphagia of benign strictures which is often intermittent. Bell's palsy is not a recognized feature of oesophageal carcinoma.

14.26 A 1982 (B) 1982 (C) 1983 (D) 1983 E 1983
There is a low incidence of gastric carcinoma in the USA, but a high incidence in Japan, parts of Chile and the mountainous region of Costa Rica. The early reports of the link between *H. pylori* and gastric carcinoma continue to be substantiated and *H. pylori* must continue to be regarded as an aetiological factor. There is no good evidence that cancer develops in a proven benign gastric ulcer. Thus benign ulcers are not premalignant. It can however be difficult to differentiate radiologically and endoscopically between malignant and benign ulcers, and malignant ulcers can heal temporarily on medical treatment. Mass screening in Japan has undoubtedly increased the proportion of early cancers diagnosed with the benefit that early action results in a five-year survival rate of about 90%. However, gastric screening is expensive. The uptake is low and generally the incidence of gastric carcinoma is declining. Most commentators therefore believe screening is unjustified except in particularly high risk people.

14.27 A 1985 B 1985 (C) 1985 (D) 1986 E 1986
The small bowel accounts for 1–5% of all gastrointestinal tract tumours, thus a small bowel cancer is 40–60 times less common than a colonic cancer. Adenocarcinoma is the most common (50%) of the small bowel malignancies followed by carcinoid tumour whilst lymphoma and smooth-muscle tumours make up the remainder. About 10–15% of patients with familial adenomatosis polyposis of the small bowel develop a malignancy, most commonly an adenocarcinoma of the Ampulla of Vater. Coeliac disease is associated with an increased incidence of adenocarcinoma and lymphoma of the small bowel, as well as with cancers throughout the gastrointestinal tract (e.g. oesophagus) and elsewhere (e.g. the testis).

14.28 (A) 1992 B 1992 C 1992 D 1992 (E) 1992
Dukes described a staging classification in 1932 for rectal carcinomas. Subsequently this was extended to colonic tumours. Modifications have been made, such as the inclusion of the extent of tumour nodal or metastatic involvement (TNM classification), or classification by histological grade but these modifications seem to have added very little to the accuracy of the

original classification. A Dukes' A tumour is one which has penetrated the muscular mucosa but not the bowel wall. Dukes' C tumours are sometimes divided into local nodal involvement (C_1) and apical nodes (C_2). The prognosis for all Dukes C tumours is not as poor as less than a 5% five-year survival. It is currently about 30–40% five-year survival for C_1 tumours and 10–20% five-year survival for C_2 tumours.

14.29 **(A)** 1996 **(B)** 1996 **C** 1997 **(D)** 1996 **(E)** 1997
The inferior mesenteric artery is rarely affected by stenotic lesions; the coeliac axis and superior mesenteric artery are the common sites. The classical cramping pain of ischaemic bowel occurs 20 minutes to 1 hour after a meal. Although angiography is helpful diagnostically, it should be emphasized that many patients with severe symptoms have no radiological findings and vice versa. Surgery certainly helps some patients but does not achieve consistently successful results. The aetiology, investigation and treatment of this syndrome needs further elucidation.

14.30 **(A)** 2005 **B** 2005 **C** 2006 **D** 2006 **E** 2006
Heavy metals, such as cadmium and arsenic, can cause diarrhoea but not zinc. Mushroom poisoning, particularly with *Amanita phalloides*, can cause severe vomiting and diarrhoea. Scromboid poisoning occurs from eating poorly refrigerated fish in which the bacteria have caused the breakdown of histine in fish muscle to saurine, a histamine-like substance. The effect of eating the fish is rather like histamine poisoning with diarrhoea, flushing, urticaria, myalgia and swelling of the tongue and throat.

14.31 **(A)** 2018 **B** 2018 **(C)** 2018 **D** 2018 **(E)** 2018
The early features of primary haemochromatosis include hepatomegaly (75–90% of patients), skin pigmentation, cardiomyopathy and joint disease but not haemolytic anaemia. A major late complication is the development of hepatocellular carcinoma in association with iron overload. The features of alpha$_1$-antitrypsin deficiency include emphysema, neonatal hepatitis and childhood cirrhosis. Porphyria is characterized by skin light sensitivity, hepatomegaly and personality changes but not pigmentation. Wilson's disease causes haemolytic anaemia, hepatic failure, fibrosis and cirrhosis with portal hypertension and neuropsychiatric symptoms like dysarthria, tremor, Parkinsonian-like features and behavioural disorders.

14.32 **A** 2027 **(B)** 2027 **(C)** 2027 **D** 2027 **E** 2027

Biliary disease and alcohol abuse account for over 80% of causes of acute pancreatitis. Iatrogenic causes include surgical or endoscopic procedures involving the Ampulla of Vater. The risk of post-ERCP pancreatitis is about 1%. Viral causes include mumps virus, Coxsackie B virus and hepatitis. Prodromal diarrhoea may be useful in differentiating viral pancreatitis from other causes in which diarrhoea is rare. The drugs commonly implicated in causing hepatitis include valproic acid, azathioprine, L-asparaginase and steroids.

14.33 **A** 2028 **(B)** 2028 **C** 2028 **(D)** 2029 **E** 2029

As many as 90% of patients with acute severe pancreatitis have vomiting in the first 12 hours of illness, sometimes of sufficient severity to cause hypotension and hypovolaemia. The patient is thirsty but is reluctant to drink because of the nausea. The pain of acute pancreatitis usually starts suddenly and is very severe. However it normally lessens in severity progressively over the subsequent 72 hours and is rarely significant beyond this time. Bowel sounds are rarely present in the early days and paralytic ileus is frequent. Nasogastric aspiration will keep the patient more comfortable, but the aspirate must be measured and appropriate fluids returned intravenously. Pyrexia is frequent. Respiratory symptoms include tachypnoea, pleural effusion and marked hypoxaemia which should be monitored by measurements of arterial oxygen saturation levels.

14.34 **(A)** 2039 **B** 2039 **C** 2039 **D** 2039 **(E)** 2039

Splenic vein thrombosis occurs as a consequence of inflammation in the tail of the pancreas. It may lead to portal hypertension and gastrointestinal bleeding. Up to one-third of patients with chronic pancreatitis develop glucose intolerance. Although the diabetes is usually manageable, hypoglycaemia is not uncommon. Diabetic retinopathy may occur if diabetes is a feature, but retinopathy due to zinc or vitamin A deficiency may also occur.

14.35 **T** 2042 **B** 2042 **C** 2042 **D** 2042 **(E)** 2042

The onset of diabetes after the age of 50 years when there is no family history of diabetes, no obesity or taking of steroids would be suggestive of pancreatic carcinoma. Peripheral oedema and thrombophlebitis are recognized presentations. Bleeding from oesophageal varices may occur as a consequence of portal hypertension resulting from splenomegaly due to portal or splenic vein compression, thrombosis or diffuse liver involvement. Icterus and scratch marks are important signs.

14.36 (A) 2049   B 2049   C 2049   D 2049   (E) 2049
Gallstones occur in over 90% of patients with acute cholecystitis. Acute cholecystitis frequently follows the impaction of a gallstone in the cystic duct leading to a rise in pressure due to continuing gallbladder secretion. The right hypochondrial pain usually improves within 12–18 hours and is usually constant in contrast to the repeated severe bouts of biliary colic. Serum bilirubin can rise modestly without there being a stone in the bile duct, although such rises should not be ignored and a stone should be sought. Ultrasound is preferred because X-rays show only 10% of stones. Antibiotics are routinely used by most doctors in the conservative treatment of acute cholecystitis. They have an important preventative role.

14.37 (A) 2056   B 2056   C 2056   (D) 2056   E 2056
A haemolytic cause for jaundice would be characterised by the absence of bilirubin in the urine, but the presence instead of excess urobilinogen. If bilirubin were to be present in the urine, common causes would include hepatitis and obstruction of the biliary system. Reticulocytosis and anaemia are inevitable consequences of haemolysis. Raised serum transaminase levels are not characteristic of haemolysis, instead they are raised in conditions such as viral hepatitis.

14.38 A 2061   (B) 2061   C 2061   (D) 2061   E 2061
Hepatitis A virus is transmitted most commonly by faecal contamination of drinking water, usually in countries with low standards of hygiene. In young people the illness is usually anicteric, but in older people the disease is severe, often accompanied by jaundice. The diagnosis is made by showing IgM anti-HAV in the patient's blood. This antibody is present within 10 days of onset of viraemia and therefore detectable at presentation in almost all cases. The IgM response is followed by an IgG antibody response that confers lifelong immunity. The icteric patient may feel obliged to go to bed because of lethargy but bedrest does not appear to accelerate recovery. The patient should be allowed to take the level of exercise of which he or she feels capable.

SECTION 15: CARDIOLOGY

15.1 **(A) 2149** **(B) 2149** **C 2149** **D 2149** **E 2149**
Phase 0 of the cardiac action potential is caused by rapid Na^+ influx which causes a rapid increase in the membrane potential. This is followed by Phase 1, representing transient K^+ ion efflux, and then a prolonged slow inward Ca^{++} ion current (Phase 2). Phase 3 is recognized as repolarization and is caused by an increase in K^+ ion conductance. Phase 4 is important in specialized conduction tissue, in which there is slow spontaneous depolarization.

15.2 **(A) 2153** **(B) 2153** **(C) 2153** **D 2153** **(E) 2153**
Atrial contraction usually contributes around 10% of ventricular filling. With the onset of ventricular contraction mitral and tricuspid valves close followed by aortic and pulmonary valve opening and then ventricular emptying. Fifty to seventy per cent of the end-diastolic ventricular volume is ejected during systole. Closure of the aortic valve precedes pulmonary valve closure. The finding of a fourth heart sound is almost always pathological regardless of age, but a third heart sound can be normal in young people.

15.3 **A 2154** **(B) 2154** **(C) 2154** **D 2154** **(E) 2154**
The a wave in the right atrium should be less than 7 and the v wave less than 5 mmHg. Normal pulmonary capillary wedge pressure should be up to 10 mmHg. The left ventricular end-diastolic pressure is usually less than 12 mmHg after atrial contraction, and equalises with left atrial pressure at end-diastole. The systemic vascular resistance, and not the pulmonary vascular resistance, is calculated by the difference between the mean aortic and right atrial pressure divided by the cardiac output.

15.4 **(A) 2167** **B 2167** **(C) 2322** **(D) 2322** **(E) 2168**
Angina is a well recognized symptom of aortic stenosis and may be caused by severe left ventricular hypertrophy in the presence of normal coronary arteries. In mitral stenosis, chest pain may occur due to right ventricular ischaemia or by coronary embolization. The frequency of myocardial infarction and sudden death has a peak in the early morning waking period. Nitrates and calcium antagonists relieve oesophageal spasm as well as angina. Tietze's syndrome is due to inflammation of the costo-chondral joints and carries a benign prognosis.

15.5 **A** **2174** **(B)** **2174** **C** **2174** **D** **2174** **(E)** **2174**
Apart from rhythm-related causes of syncope, obstruction of right or left ventricular outflow (aortic stenosis, pulmonary stenosis, hypertrophic cardiomyopathy, etc.), left atrial ball valve thrombus and left atrial myxoma can also cause syncope. Other recognized causes include aortic dissection, Takayasu's disease, subclavian steal syndrome, pulmonary hypertension, cardiac tamponade and pulmonary embolism. Cerebrovascular disease should also not be forgotten as a cause of syncope.

15.6 **(A)** **2178** **B** **2178** **(C)** **2180** **D** **2181** **(E)** **2182**
The right heart border of the chest X-ray is formed by the superior vena cava, the right atrium and the inferior vena cava. The normal right ventricle lies anteriorly and does not form the right or left heart border. The left atrium is the most posterior structure of the heart and also contributes to the left heart border. In pulmonary hypertension the central pulmonary arteries are enlarged but there is evidence of peripheral pruning. Pulmonary oligaemia is typical of Fallot's tetralogy. Coronary calcification can be seen on a chest X-ray especially in elderly patients and does not necessarily imply significant coronary artery stenosis.

15.7 **A** **2185** **(B)** **2185** **C** **2185** **D** **2185** **(E)** **2186**
An inverted T wave is normal in V1 in 20% of adults, but is almost invariably abnormal when present in V4–V6. The maximum QRS duration must not exceed 100 msecs (2½ small squares). The normal frontal axis is between –30° and +90°.

15.8 **A** **2227** **B** **2227** **C** **2227** **D** **2227** **E** **2227**
There are many causes of a false positive exercise test. These include dilated and hypertrophic cardiomyopathy, hypertension or any cause of left ventricular hypertrophy. Conduction abnormalities, especially left bundle branch block and the Wolff-Parkinson-White syndrome, also cause a false positive exercise test response. Mitral valve prolapse is a recognized cause of a false positive exercise test. Drugs that may influence the interpretation of an exercise ECG response include digoxin and lithium.

15.9 **A** **2237** **(B)** **2237** **C** **2237** **(D)** **2237** **(E)** **2230**
Whilst milrinone improves ejection fraction in patients with heart failure it does so at the cost of decreased survival. Low sodium is a poor prognostic

sign as is the presence of frequent ventricular ectopics or non-sustained ventricular tachycardia. Cardiac output can be normal or even high in heart failure and is usually well preserved at rest even in severe heart failure.

15.10 **A** 2247 **(B)** 2247 **C** 2247 **(D)** 2247 **(E)** 2247
Angiotensin converting enzyme inhibitors have been shown to improve prognosis in heart failure as has the combination of nitrates and hydralazine. Prazosin and nifedipine do not, however, confer prognostic benefit and verapamil can exacerbate heart failure.

15.11 **(A)** 2234 **B** 2234 **(C)** 2234 **(D)** 2234 **E** 2235
Several adaptive mechanisms are initiated in heart failure. Vagal tone is reduced and sympathetic activation increased. Plasma antidiuretic hormone levels are usually increased as are levels of plasma insulin and atrial natruretic peptide. Increased levels of renin and angiotensin II are also present. Thyroid hormone handling is affected with a rise in reverse T3 levels. A rise in haemoglobin also occurs, probably due to chronic tissue hypoxia and a rise in erythropoietin production.

15.12 **A** 2240 **B** 2240 **C** 2240 **(D)** 2240 **(E)** 2240
Diuretic therapy, particularly thiazides, causes diabetes, gout and hypercalcaemia. Magnesium and potassium levels are often reduced. Hyponatraemia is a common finding, it is almost never due to sodium depletion but reflects water overload.

15.13 **(A)** 2256 **B** 2256 **(C)** 2256 **(D)** 2256 **(E)** 2256
Previous surgery and presensitization to HLA antigens are not absolute contraindications to cardiac transplantation, however a PVR of >8 Wood units is. HLA-DR antigen matching is desirable but not essential. Donors over 50 years old are acceptable if the coronary arteries are normal.

15.14 **(A)** 2263 **B** 2263 **C** 2263 **(D)** 2263 **E** 2263
Lignocaine is a class IB anti-arrhythmic, while racemic sotalol is a beta-blocker (class II) but with class III activity as well. The d-isomer of sotalol has only class III activity. Class III agents prolong the action potential. Propafenone is a class IC agent but has some beta-blocking activity. Digoxin and adenosine are not classified within the Vaughan Williams classification.

15.15 A 2272 **(B)** 2272 **(C)** 2272 **(D)** 2272 **(E)** 2272
Atrial fibrillation can be caused by ventricular pacing. The risk of stroke is increased by five-fold with chronic atrial fibrillation and can be up to 17-fold in rheumatic mitral stenosis. Paroxysmal atrial fibrillation, however, has a lower risk than persistent atrial fibrillation. Calcium antagonists, such as verapamil, can be used to control the ventricular rate, as can beta-blockers either alone or in combination with digoxin. When atrial fibrillation is caused by thyrotoxicosis, the latter should be treated first before attempting cardioversion. Beta-blockers are particularly useful in controlling the ventricular rate as well as the symptoms of thyrotoxicosis.

15.16 (A) 2277 **B** 2276 **(C)** 2277 **D** 2277 **E** 2277
An accessory pathway can be present even with a normal ECG (known as a concealed pathway). Atrial fibrillation represents the main risk of sudden death if it is conducted 1:1 down an accessory pathway causing ventricular fibrillation. Not all accessory pathways are capable of conducting so rapidly and conduction through the pathway slows with advancing age. Wolf-Parkinson-White syndrome is associated with Ebstein's anomaly (in which there are varying degrees of tricuspid valve abnormality), hypertrophic cardiomyopathy and mitral valve prolapse.

15.17 (A) 2284 **(B)** 2284 **C** 2284 **(D)** 2284 **(E)** 2284
Of all the causes of cardiac arrest, ventricular fibrillation carries the best prognosis. The dose of adrenaline is 1 mg intravenously. Three DC shocks should be given for ventricular fibrillation before drug therapy is started. There is no evidence that mannitol improves cerebral recovery after cardiac arrest. Long-term survival of survivors of cardiac arrest after hospital discharge is between 50–60% at 5 years.

15.18 (A) 2296 **(B)** 2296 **C** 2296 **D** 2296 **E** 2296
Nitric oxide is synthesized from L-arginine in endothelial cells and other tissues. It has a half-life of only a few seconds and is rapidly inactivated by haemoglobin. Nitric oxide production is stimulated by sheer stress, aggregating platelets, acetylcholine, bradykinin and substance P.

15.19 A 2305 **(B)** 2306 **(C)** 2308 **D** 2315 **(E)** 2314
The annual incidence rate of ischaemic heart disease in Finland is 198/

10,000 compared with 15/10,000 in Japan. However, migrants from low-risk to high-risk countries tend to acquire the increased risk. Lipoprotein alpha levels are higher in patients with atherosclerosis and lipoprotein alpha may have thrombogenic and atherogenic effects. Mortality from ischaemic heart disease is greater in the winter months. Hormone replacement therapy decreases the risk of ischaemic heart disease by about 0.5 of the relative risk.

15.20 A 2325   B 2325   C 2325   D 2325   E 2325
Coronary emboli can cause myocardial ischaemia and infarction, arising from both subacute bacterial endocarditis and an atrial myxoma. Procoagulable states such as protein C deficiency can cause myocardial ischaemia and infarction as a result of spontaneous coronary thrombosis. Hypertrophic cardiomyopathy can cause ischaemia as a result of dynamic obstruction to left ventricular outflow. Syndrome X describes patients with normal coronaries and positive exercise tests. Some of these have ischaemia due to microvascular disease.

15.21 (A) 2377   (B) 2378   C 2379   D 2377   E 2379
Takayasu's disease is a panarteritis of the aorta and its main branches and of the pulmonary arteries. Patients are typically young females of Oriental origin and can present with a prodromal phase of generalized malaise, associated with syncopal attacks. Retinopathy is well recognized as is hypertension, aortic regurgitation and aortic aneurysm. Steroid treatment reduces the progression of arterial involvement especially in those with evidence of active inflammation.

15.22 A 2385   B 2385   C 2384   (D) 2387   E 2387
Hypertrophic cardiomyopathy is transmitted in an autosomal dominant fashion with variable penetrance. Mutations in genes including beta cardiac myosin heavy chain, alpha tropomyosin and cardiac troponin T have been described. Isolated right ventricular hypertrophy is rare, although it is present in conjunction with left ventricular hypertrophy in over 30%. Hypertrophy often increases during growth spurts, but is not progressive in nature in adult life and does not develop *de novo* in adult life. The intensity of the ejection systolic murmur is increased by manoeuvres that decrease venous return or afterload (amyl nitrate, standing, Valsalva) and decreased by an increase in venous return or afterload (squatting, phenylephrine).

15.23 **(A)** 2392 **(B)** 2392 **(C)** 2392 **D** 2392 **E** 2392
Clinical cardiac involvement in systemic lupus erythematosus (SLE) is seen in 50–60%, but death from cardiac causes is rare. Myocarditis and endocarditis are often subclinical and rarely result in cardiac failure or significant regurgitation. Libman-Sachs is a non-infective endocarditis. High titres of antiphospholipid antibodies are associated with cardiac and particularly valvular involvement.

15.24 **A** 2394 **B** 2395 **(C)** 2395 **D** 2395 **(E)** 2396
The heart is involved in up to 50% of patients with AIDS, but only causes symptoms in 10%, and death in less than 5%. Dilated cardiomyopathy is the commonest clinical cardiological manifestation in the West, although isolated right ventricular dilatation can occur. Cardiac Kaposi's sarcoma rarely causes cardiac death or significant morbidity. Zidovudine does not improve cardiac function in AIDS and should be withdrawn in patients with severe heart failure as it may be cardiotoxic.

15.25 **(A)** 2400 **B** 2400 **C** 2401 **(D)** 2401 **E** 2402
Venesection in patients with congenital heart disease should always be accompanied by fluid replacement but this should be colloid as normal saline can precipitate thrombosis. Both gout and hypertrophic osteoarthropathy can occur. Patients may be 'anaemic' and iron deficient despite a normal haemoglobin. High oestrogen oral contraception is contraindicated due to an increased risk of thrombosis.

15.26 **A** 2402 **(B)** 2402 **(C)** 2402 **D** 2402 **E** 2402
Fallot's tetralogy is the combination of a large subaortic VSD, infundibular stenosis, an overriding aorta, and right ventricular hypertrophy. Clinically, there is cyanosis, right ventricular hypertrophy, a single (aortic) second heart sound and a pulmonary ejection systolic murmur. Aortic regurgitation and right heart failure can occur, but this is usually in adult life.

15.27 **(A)** 2425 **(B)** 2425 **C** 2425 **D** 2427 **(E)** 2426
Ostium secundum defects are the most common. They rarely give rise to symptoms until adulthood. By middle age there is a high incidence of atrial fibrillation and disabling symptoms. Ostium primum defects are rarer and associated with mitral valve abnormalities. The ECG characteristically shows left axis deviation in ostium primum defects and right axis deviation in ostium secundum defects.

15.28 A   2434   (B)   2434   C   2434   (D)   2434   E   2434
The major criteria according to the revised Jones criteria are carditis, polyarthritis, chorea, erythema marginatum and subcutaneous nodules. Minor criteria include previous rheumatic fever or rheumatic heart disease, arthralgia, a raised ESR or C reactive protein, a raised white cell count, and a prolonged PR interval on the ECG.

15.29 (A)   2452   B   2452   (C)   2453   D   2453   E   2455
Patients with symptomatic mitral stenosis have a valve area of 0.75–1.25 cm^2. Angina can occur as a result of coronary embolisation or due to severe right ventricular hypertrophy. Splenic infarction can also result from embolization to the splenic artery in the absence of endocarditis. A short diastolic murmur indicates mild stenosis. Cor triatrium (extra membrane within the left atrium) or left atria myxoma can have identical signs to that of mitral stenosis.

15.30 A   2457   B   2458   C   2457   (D)   2457   E   2459
Mitral regurgitation can result from a floppy mitral valve and is seen in Marfan's syndrome, pseudoxanthoma elasticum, Ehlers Danlos syndrome and osteogenesis imperfecta. Dilatation of the mitral ring can also cause regurgitation secondary to a dilated cardiomyopathy (for example caused by alcohol) and in acute myocarditis. Papillary muscle rupture secondary to myocardial infarction can also result in mitral regurgitation. Mitral regurgitation is relatively common in hypertrophic cardiomyopathy in the presence of systolic anterior movement (SAM) of the anterior mitral valve leaflet.

15.31 (A)   2462   B   2462   C   2462   (D)   2464   (E)   2463
Aortic stenosis due to a bicuspid aortic valve is not usually symptomatic until adult life. Although a normal ECG can be present in severe aortic stenosis, left ventricular hypertrophy is far more common. Ventricular arrhythmias and heart block have a well recognized association with aortic stenosis. Balloon valvuloplasty, although effective in childhood, is largely ineffective in adults especially with the development of calcification.

15.32 A   2465   B   2465   (C)   2465   (D)   2465   (E)   2465
Ulcerative colitis, ankylosing spondylitis and rheumatoid arthritis have a well recognized association with aortic regurgitation. Subaortic ventricular

septal defects can also be associated with aortic regurgitation due to loss of support of the valve ring. De Mussett's sign is nodding of the head due to a large aortic impulse and Durosiez's sign is the presence of a diastolic murmur in the femoral artery heard proximally after compression of the femoral artery. Although a short diastolic murmur is present in mild aortic regurgitation, in severe acute cases the murmur is also short due to a rapid rise in left ventricular diastolic pressure. An ejection systolic murmur is common in aortic regurgitation due to increased flow and does not imply the presence of aortic stenosis.

15.33 A 2506 B 2506 C 2506 D 2506 E 2506
Hypoxia at high altitude can cause pulmonary hypertension. Amniotic fluid embolism can also cause pulmonary hypertension as can hepatic cirrhosis usually in relation to porto-systemic shunting. Sickle cell disease can cause pulmonary hypertension due to repeated sickle crisis. Denatured rape seed oil can cause toxin mediated pulmonary hypertension.

15.34 (A) 2557 (B) 2557 C 2557 D 2557 E 2559
Coarctation of the aorta is most commonly found distal to the left subclavian artery, in either the pre- or post-ductal position, and is usually more severe when present in the pre-ductal position. They are more common in males and have an association with bicuspid aortic valves and floppy mitral valves. Noonan's and Turner's syndrome have a well recognized association with coarctation. Surgical repair can be complicated by paraplegia, mesenteric ischaemia and paradoxical hypertension.

SECTION 16: INTENSIVE CARE

16.1 A 2563 B 2563 C 2563 D 2563 E 2563
The internal jugular vein has the advantage that the position of the catheter does not require radiographic confirmation. Pneumothorax is a small risk for the subclavian approach. Pressure within the circulation needs to be measured from a fixed point, usually the sternal angle. Acute myocardial infarction and diabetic ketoacidosis is one combination which can result in heart failure without a raised CVP. With a high CVP an inotropic agent is usually needed, preferable one which does not raise

system resistance. Dopamine or dobutamine are two possibilities. In patients with a low CVP the right-atrial pressure needs restoration with a plasma expander. If then a normal right-atrial pressure fails to produce a normal circulation, an inotrope may be needed to boost the heart.

16.2 **A 2576** **B 2576** **C 2576** **D 2576** **E 2576**
Almost all patients with pneumonia can be maintained on a ventilator at a level that will sustain their respiratory functions, though they may die from the toxic effect of the infection on other organs. An uncontrolled flail segment of the chest wall will inevitably be complicated by collapse and consolidation as well as impairing the efficiency of respiration by its paradoxical movement. These complications can be prevented either by wiring or by positive-pressure ventilation. The considerable respiratory workload caused by pulmonary oedema (in addition to its deleterious effect on gas exchange) makes this condition particularly susceptible to treatment with positive-pressure ventilation. Cerebral oedema following head injury or cardiac arrest may be treated or prevented by a period of hyperventilation on a ventilator. The purpose is to reduce carbon dioxide tension to values between 3.3 and 4.0 kPa which has the effect of reducing cerebral blood flow to control the oedema. A cardiac output of less than 2 l/min in a 70 kg patient or a cardiac index of less than 1.2 l/m^2 is an indication for ventilatory support.

16.3 **(A) 2582** **B 2582** **(C) 2582** **D 2582** **(E) 2582**
The oculocephalic responses are tested by rotating the patient's head rapidly from one side to another while keeping the eyelids open. If the patient is unconscious the eyes will initially be 'left behind' but will then catch up and come to occupy their original resting position relative to the skull. The movements elicited in this way are known as doll's head eye movements. They are dependent upon the presence of functioning long tracts. Deviation of both eyes towards the irrigated ear following caloric stimulation indicates an intact brain stem. The ciliospinal reflex is a homolateral pupillary dilation caused by pinching of the skin of the neck. The corneal reflexes test the integrity of the Vth and VIIth cranial nerves.

SECTION 17: RESPIRATORY MEDICINE

17.1 **(A) 2594   B 2596   (C) 2601   D 2613   E 2613**
There is a rapid fall in the air velocity towards the periphery of the lung allowing diffusion of oxygen into the red blood cell. Under resting conditions, only one-tenth of the amount of oxygen is taken up by the lungs. Surfactant prevents the lung from collapsing with resultant alveolar closure. The surface film moves from the alveolus to the bronchioles thus carrying small particles, damaged cells and other debris towards the mucociliary escalator. Surfactant also contains several protective immunoglobulins, and there is evidence that it exerts a variety of influences on alveolar macrophages including chemotaxis and enhanced killing.

17.2 **A 2633   B 2643   C 2666   (D) 2667   E 2668**
The VC is greater than the FVC in obstruction due to gas trapping. The increased sputum DNA content associated with infection is responsible for the increased viscosity of the sputum, hence the rationale of trials using DNAses in the treatment of suppurative lung infections. FRC is increased as a proportion of TLC in obstruction. The last part of expiration is not effort-dependent and is related to lung recoil and compliance. Capsaicin is believed to stimulate bronchial C fibres which are thought to mediate the cough reflex.

17.3 **(A) 2697   B 2697   (C) 2696   (D) 2694   E 2695**
Sputum microscopy is far superior to culture. However, although its specificity is high its sensitivity is low. Moreover, the value of sputum culture in the diagnosis of atypical pneumonia is limited as mycoplasma is the only organism that can be grown with any ease albeit with special media and taking several weeks. To make a diagnosis using serological methods, a four-fold or greater change in specific antibody titre is accepted as evidence of recent infection. Crepitations are the most frequently encountered signs of pneumonia.

17.4 **(A) 2714   (B) 2714   (C) 2715   D 2715   E 2718**
The incidence of allergic rhinitis is increasing for reasons that are unclear. One possible factor is the effect of atmospheric pollution. *Dermatophagoides pteronyssinus* is the cause of perennial allergic rhinitis. The allergen is a cysteine protease which is present in high concentration in mite faeces. The

immediate symptoms of allergic rhinitis occur as a consequence of type I immediate hypersensitivity. Further chronic inflammation is orchestrated by cytokines produced by TH2 type helper T lymphocytes. TH2 type cells mainly produce IL-4 and IL-5. IL-4 is the major cytokine responsible for B-cell IgE production. IL-5 and granulocyte-macrophage stimulating factor are important in the proliferation of eosinophils.

17.5 **(A)** 2725 **(B)** 2726 **C** 2726 **(D)** 2727 **(E)** 2727
Methacholine causes smooth muscle contraction and is a measure of the non-specific reactivity which is characteristic of asthma and correlates with disease severity. Other chemical stimuli act indirectly by inducing the release of mast cell mediators such as adenosine. There is accumulating evidence in the literature implicating T-cells in the pathogenesis of asthma. T-cells present in asthmatic biopsies are activated with an increased ability to secrete inflammatory cytokines. Extrinsic asthma is characterized by a clear provocation by recognized allergens usually affecting younger individuals under the age of 30.

17.6 **(A)** 2728 **B** 2730 **C** 2731 **D** 2732 **E** 2735
Airflow obstruction is due mainly to small airways dysfunction. Allergic asthmatic individuals may develop a late phase response following allergen exposure characterised by increased non-specific responsiveness and an accumulation of inflammatory cells. Exercise-induced asthma is characterized by worsening of symptoms after exercise has finished. It can be prevented by either a beta-2 agonist or disodium cromoglycate. The asthma triad as described by Samter includes asthma, nasal polyps and aspirin intolerance. As many as 2% of asthmatics suffer from this disorder.

17.7 **(A)** 2746 **B** 2749 **(C)** 2755 **(D)** 2752 **E** 2753
The cystic fibrosis gene is located on the long arm of chromosome 7 and is known as the cystic fibrosis transmembrane conductance regulator (CFTR). The CFTR has been shown to transport chloride ions which, when disrupted, results in deficient water transport into, and deficient sodium reabsorption from, mucus. This leads to increased mucus viscosity. Atopy is seen in a high proportion of CF patients (88%) and is associated with clinical asthma. In the early stages of the disease, infecting organisms are usually of a conventional type. As the disease advances, *Pseudomonas* becomes a more important and difficult pathogen to treat.

17.8 **A** 2761 **B** 2761 **(C)** 2763 **(D)** 2761 **E** 2758
Although the sputum may be colonized by *Pseudomonas*, it has a clinically significant effect in only a small proportion of patients with bronchiectasis. The most frequently isolated organisms are pneumococcus and *H. influenzae* (75%). Bronchiectasis is usually widespread and only confined in certain situations, such as following inhalation of foreign bodies and lobar pneumonia. Deficiencies of IgG2 and IgG4 are particularly associated with bronchiectasis.

17.9 **(A)** 2776 **(B)** 2776 **C** 2777 **D** 2776 **E** 2776
Ipratropium bromide (Atrovent) is as good a bronchodilator as salbutamol in patients with chronic obstructive pulmonary disease (COPD). Advanced cases of COPD are often associated with severe weight loss which is not necessarily associated with an underlying malignancy. In patients with COPD, because the PaO_2 is reduced and close to the steep part of the oxygen dissociation curve, the usual small fall in oxygen saturation during sleep leads to a much greater fall in oxygen saturation. Present guidelines recommend long-term oxygen treatment for more than 15 hours per day when PaO_2 is less than 7.3 kPa (55 mm Hg). Survival has been shown to be enhanced and hospital admissions reduced. A formal steroid trial consists of 40 mg of prednisolone for 2–3 weeks with spirometry performed before and after steroid treatment.

17.10 **A** 2786 **B** 2780 **C** 2791 **D** 2792 **E** 2793
Cryptogenic fibrosing alveolitis (CFA) is a disease associated with 50% mortality at 5 years. A clear tissue diagnosis may not be mandatory particularly in the elderly with poor lung function. It would be more important in the younger patient in whom a precise diagnosis would allow the therapeutic options to be carefully considered and discussed with the patient. High resolution CT of the thorax is the imaging technique of choice in the assessment of diffuse interstitial lung disease. The pattern of abnormality may be pathognomonic and may obviate the need for biopsy. The response to treatment is usually poor. Objective response rates of 20% are evident with steroids or steroids in combination with cyclophosphamide.

17.11 **(A)** 2782 **(B)** 2782 **C** 2782 **(D)** 2782 **(E)** 2782
Clubbing is rarely associated with extrinsic allergic alveolitis (EAA). There

is no temporal relationship between rheumatoid arthritis and fibrosing alveolitis and it can occur at any time either before or after the onset of joint symptoms. Asbestosis usually produces lower lobe shadowing. Diagnostic material may be obtained in some disease processes such as alveolar proteinosis (lipoproteinaceous material) and histiocytosis X (Langerhans cells). Anti-DNA topoisomerase antibodies is associated with diffuse systemic sclerosis which is associated with pulmonary fibrosis and pulmonary vascular disease.

17.12 **(A)** **2894** **(B)** **2894** **(C)** **2783** **(D)** **2893** **(E)** **2893**
Asbestos-related diseases will continue to emerge after exposure due to the long latency of up to 40 years. The incidence is still rising in the UK. Although there is usually good evidence of previous asbestos exposure, it has been estimated that the annual incidence of patients who develop a mesothelioma with no previous exposure is about 1 per million. There is good epidemiological evidence that crocidolite (blue asbestos) is more hazardous than chrysotile (white asbestos). Mesothelioma is extremely difficult to treat with no curative therapy. The prognosis is poor with a median survival of 18 months.

17.13 **A** **2796** **(B)** **2798** **C** **2799** **(D)** **2799** **(E)** **2797**
There are two important forms of bronchiolitis obliterans of which BOOP is more responsive to treatment.The shrinking lung syndrome is associated with diaphragmatic dysfunction and reduced pressures. The principal muscle for respiration is the diaphragm and this is not involved in ankylosing spondylitis, thus a frozen thorax causes little respiratory embarrassment. Better differentiation between exudates and transudates include the use of fluid-to-serum ratio of total protein (> 0.5) and lactic dehydrogenase levels (> 0.6), and fluid lactic dehydrogenase concentrations greater than 200 IU.

17.14 **A** **2800** **(B)** **2803** **C** **2801** **(D)** **2802** **E** **2800**
Churg Strauss syndrome is characterized by asthma, eosinophilia greater than $1.5 \times 10^9/l$ and systemic vasculitis. The upper respiratory tract features in contrast to Wegener's granulomatosis is 'allergic' rather than vasculitic or granulomatous.Goodpasture's syndrome involves pulmonary haemorrhage and glomerulonephritis with the demonstration of autoantibodies to the alpha-3 chain of type IV collagen of

the glomerular basement membrane. Bronchocentric granulomatosis is a disorder predominantly centred around the airways producing localized pulmonary shadowing with persisting cough and dyspnoea.

17.15   **A   2804   (B)   2821   C   2805   (D)   2811   (E)   2830**
Lofgren's syndrome is the classical presentation of sarcoidosis with erythema nodosum and bihilar lymphadenopathy. It should not be confused with Loffler's syndrome which is the syndrome of transitory migratory pulmonary shadows due to an eosinophilic alveolar exudate and peripheral eosinophilia. Allergic bronchopulmonary aspergillosis consists of asthma and fleeting pulmonary infiltrates with a tendency to damage the bronchial wall leading to proximal bronchiectasis. *Aspergillus* sensitivity accounts for more than 90% cases of pulmonary eosinophilia in the United Kingdom. Sarcoidosis and extrinsic allergic alveolitis are associated with lymphocytic infiltration of the lung.

17.16   **(A)   2811   (B)   2814   (C)   2810   D   2811   E   2809**
There is little evidence for the previously held view that extrinsic allergic alveolitis (EAA) is a type III hypersensitivity reaction. EAA is most commonly caused by *Micropolyspora faeni* and is called Farmer's lung. Respiratory distress with fever and basal crackles are the major clinical features with spontaneous recovery expected within 12–24 hours. Histology is indicated only when other diagnostic procedures are not sufficient but is rarely needed. The most characteristic feature is the formation of non-caseating granulomas. When the diagnosis is in doubt, some form of inhalational test may be required.

17.17   **(A)   2819   B   2819   C   2820   (D)   2821   E   2819**
Sarcoidosis is a systemic granulomatous disorder in which there is an increased CD4 helper T-lymphocyte response maintained by several cytokines. CD4 cells accumulate at the site of active involvement and studies have demonstrated an CD4:CD8 ratio as high as 10:1. Uveoparotid fever syndrome is an uncommon form of presentation. Direct granulomatous involvement of the myocardium is found in up to 20% of cases. Arrhythmias, heart failure and pericarditis are the usual modes of presentation, valvular lesions are uncommon.

17.18 (A) 2884   B 2889   C 2889   (D) 2891   (E) 2885
Lung malignancies are separated into essentially two groups, small cell lung cancer and other tumours. Small cell tumours disseminate early in the course of their natural history and are usually inoperable. They are also more sensitive to chemotherapeutic agents, which improve survival from 6 weeks to 12 months in extensive disease. The total response rate is in the order of 80%. The TNM classification is used in the staging of non-small cell lung cancer and prognosis is related to the tumour size, number of histologically affected nodes and presence of metastases. The staging for small cell lung cancer is simply designated by extension outside the thorax and ipsilateral supraclavicular lymph nodes.

17.19 A 2902   (B) 2903   C 2904   D 2904   E 2903
The alveolar-arterial (A-a) gradient gives an indication of the severity of impaired oxygenation by the lung. Ventilatory capacity is measured by use of spirometry and exercise testing. Respiratory failure is usually divided into type 1 or type 2. Type 1 respiratory failure represents oxygenation failure including pneumonia and pulmonary fibrosis. Type 2 ventilatory failure results from the complex interrelationship between three components: ventilatory drive, the capacity of the respiratory pump, and the load imposed on the ventilatory system. Examples of type 2 failure include central alveolar hypoventilation (ventilatory drive), thoracic cage deformities (respiratory pump) and obstructive sleep apnoea (load imposed on respiratory pump).

17.20 A 2912   (B) 2910   (C) 2914   D 2909   E 2911
Obstructive sleep apnoea is a common respiratory disorder affecting 1% of males. It is associated with obesity; the majority of patients are overweight. Oronasal factors are extremely important and may be correctable. Although the main reason for treating OSA is to relieve the daytime symptoms, there is evidence that untreated these patients have an increased cardiovascular mortality. The treatment is with nasal CPAP often with dramatic response. Unfortunately, this condition is lifelong unless the patient is able to lose a significant amount of weight. The role of surgery in the treatment of OSA is not yet clearly established.

17.21 A 2933   (B) 2934   C 2937   D 2937   E 2936
Lung transplantation is usually offered when there are no further therapeutic options and it offers a survival advantage. The choice of the procedure is

governed by the type of lung disease with heart–lung transplantation the procedure of choice in cases of primary pulmonary hypertension. The improvement in quality of life depends largely on lung function and exercise capacity. Double lung transplant recipients achieve better exercise performance than heart–lung recipients as a result of better cardiac performance. The major limitations on improvements of exercise tolerance are the presence of acute rejection or the development of bronchiolitis obliterans.

SECTION 18: RHEUMATOLOGY

18.1 **A 2970 (B) 2970 C 2971 (D) 2961 E 2971**
There are numerous features of reactive arthritis which may encompass arthritis, conjunctivitis and urethritis, plus circinate balanitis, anterior uveitis, oral ulcers, keratoderma blennorrhagica and enthesitis. Any of these features may develop 3–30 days after the precipitating infection.

18.2 **A 2955 (B) 2955 C 2955 (D) 2955 E 2955**
Rheumatoid arthritis (RA) typically causes a peripheral, symmetrical, small-joint polyarthritis involving the proximal interphalangeal and metacarpophalangeal joints of the hands, the metatarsophalangeal joints, the wrists, ankles and cervical spine. RA has a peak incidence in the fifth decade but can occur at any age. The onset is insidious in up to 70% of cases, and is associated with a poor prognosis. About 10% of cases have a very rapid onset, even overnight. Such patients often have a better outcome than might be expected. RA affects women more than men with a lifetime incidence in women three times that of men. The sex difference is most apparent in early onset disease and has almost disappeared by the age of 65. Erosion of articular cartilage is one of the characteristic pathological developments in RA and is responsible for the loss of joint space on X-ray which is one of the diagnostic features of RA.

18.3 **A 2984 B 2985 (C) 2985 D 2985 (E) 2987**
The first acute attack of gout usually affects a single peripheral joint, specifically the first metatarsophalangeal joint in 50% of cases. If left untreated symptoms resolve spontaneously over 5–15 days, often with pruritus and desquamation of overlying skin. Most hyperuricaemic patients never develop gout which emphasizes the importance of local tissue factors in the aetiology of crystal formation. Some gouty patients are not

hyperuricaemic at presentation. Men with ischaemic heart disease have an increased chance of gout, but not women. Most patients with primary gout have inherited an isolated renal lesion that reduces fractional urate clearance and are undersecretors of uric acid. The treatment of choice is allopurinol but it does not have frequent side-effects in elderly people. Renal, gut and nervous system side-effects in elderly people are more characteristic of indomethacin.

18.4 A 2998 B 2998 (C) 2998 (D) 2998 (E) 2998
Joints are most commonly infected by the haematogenous spread of micro-organisms from a remote site such as the nose, middle ear, lungs, rectum, or urethra. Malignancy, diabetes mellitus, alcoholism and anaemia are some of the predisposing causes of septic arthritis. *Haemophilus influenzae* is the most likely causative organism in children under 2 years of age, *Staphylococcus* is more commonly found in older children and in patients with rheumatoid arthritis. The knee is the most commonly infected joint. The infected joint should be aspirated for diagnostic purposes and to relieve pain, but intra-articular antibiotics are not indicated. They can cause a chemical synovitis and may even introduce further infection. Maximum serum and synovial fluid concentrations of antibiotics can be achieved by parenteral administration.

18.5 (A) 3001 B 3001 C 3001 D 3000 (E) 3000
Arthritis is not a well recognized feature of measles but it does occur, particularly in young males, in mumps. The arthritis is migratory, lasts 2 weeks and leaves no permanent damage. A polyarticular, symmetrical arthritis of smaller joints affects about one-half of patients with hepatitis B. It appears with the prodromal features and may last from a few days to several weeks. Coccidioidomycosis occurs in south-western USA and Mexico. In about one-third of patients there is an arthritis plus erythema nodosum, fever and malaise. There is no residual damage. Arthritis is not a feature of trichomonas.

18.6 A 3018 (B) 3037 C 3014 (D) 3038 E 3012
Glomerulonephritis is probably the most common cause of death in patients with systemic lupus erythematosus. It may, however, be a complication of uraemia, such as infection, that is the final cause of death since dialysis and effective treatments for hypertension and dialysis are now available. The

onset may be acute or with asymptomatic haematuria or proteinuria. Nephritis is not a feature of polymyositis or giant cell arteritis. Proteinuria, haematuria, or malignant hypertension are possible presenting features of polyarteritis nodosa. Progression to renal failure was an important cause of death before renal replacement therapy was available. In Wegener's granulomatosis the prognosis is largely determined by the extent and progress of renal disease. Acute focal necrotizing glomerular capillaritis with crescent formation is the hallmark of rapidly progressive disease.

18.7 **A 3041** **(B) 3042** **C 3042** **(D) 3042** **E 3042**
Giant-cell (cranial, senile or temporal) arteritis mainly affects people aged 65–75 years and is rare before the age of 50. The onset of symptoms may be very sudden and the condition is nearly always fully developed within a few weeks although diagnosis may take months. A 2 cm segment of tender temporal artery obtained under local anaesthetic will provide a definite diagnosis in about 70% of cases and is the definitive test. A longer segment or biopsy of more than one tender arteries may enhance the success rate. Recurrence of symptoms, even blindness, may occur after successful treatment with corticosteroids so follow-up should be meticulous and the patient warned to re-present promptly should symptoms recur. Despite all its complications giant-cell arteritis does not reduce life expectancy.

18.8 **(A) 3027** **(B) 3027** **C 3027** **D 3027** **E 3027**
Neither rubber nor asbestos are associated with scleroderma. Silica, however, is implicated, particularly in stonemasons, coalminers and goldminers. Silicone, augmentation mammoplasty and paraffin are implicated as well as the drugs cocaine, L-tryptophan, bleomycin, pentazocine and some appetite suppressants. Other agents implicated include epoxy resins, organic chemicals such as aliphatic hydrocarbons (e.g. vinyl chloride) or aromatic hydrocarbons (e.g. benzene).

18.9 **(A) 3019** **B 3019** **C 3019** **D 3020** **E 3020**
The skin is a target organ in over 70% of patients with systemic lupus erythematosus (SLE) but keloid scarring is not one of the manifestations. Rashes, alopecia and photosensitivity are the associated dermatological features. Nephritis is still probably the most common cause of death, although with good treatment for hypertension and effective dialysis the mortality has been greatly reduced. For these reasons urinalysis is crucial

to the diagnosis, assessment and management of patients with lupus. Twenty to thirty per cent of SLE patients have Raynaud's phenomenon compared to up to 15% of the general population. The most common haematological feature of SLE is a normocytic, normochromic or hypochromic anaemia. However an immune thrombocytopenia is well recognized and may indeed be the presenting feature. Basal atelectasis progressing to 'shrinking lungs' is one of the respiratory features of SLE.

SECTION 19: DISORDERS OF THE SKELETON

19.1 **(A)** **3055** **B** **3055** **C** **3055** **D** **3055** **E** **3055**
Osteoblasts have a central role in bone function. They are derived from the mesenchymal stromal cell system. The haemopoietic system, by contrast, provides osteoclasts which have a phagocytic function in bone resorption. Osteoblasts synthesize the bone matrix, mainly collagen, and they control bone mineralization. They appear to control the activity of other cell types, particularly the osteoclast, and thus may activate the bone resorbing cycle. Osteoblasts are activated by parathyroid hormone and 1, 25-hydroxycholecalciferol.

19.2 **(A)** **3063** **B** **3063** **(C)** **3063** **D** **3063** **E** **3063**
The main determinant of the fasting plasma phosphate concentration is the rate of renal tubular reabsorption. Hypophosphataemia therefore occurs in primary hyperparathyroidism, in the humoral hypercalcaemia of malignancy and in inherited hypophosphataemic rickets. Prolonged intravenous nutrition and oral aluminium hydroxide are other causes of low plasma phosphate. By contrast hyperphosphataemia occurs in hypoparathyroidism and in renal glomerular failure.

19.3 **A** **3065** **(B)** **3065** **(C)** **3065** **D** **3065** **E** **3065**
Bone mass reaches a peak at about 30 years of age and is higher in men than women. From this age bone is then progressively lost in men at a steady rate and in women rapidly after the menopause for about 10 years and then at the same rate as men. The rate of bone loss is increased by smoking, alcohol, thinness, immobility, hysterectomy, early natural or surgically induced menopause and episodes of amenorrhoea in early life.

19.4 **(A) 3071** **B 3071** **(C) 3071** **D 3071** **E 3071**
In osteomalacia the linear growth rate is reduced causing bowing of the long bones, but this is characteristically accompanied by pain. The main symptoms of osteomalacia are bony pain and proximal muscle weakness. The cause of this weakness is unknown and its severity varies with different forms of osteomalacia. A waddling gait, difficulty getting up and down stairs and out of low chairs are the common consequences. Vertebral collapse is not a recognized feature of osteomalacia (but it is of osteoporosis) although severe osteomalacia may cause kyphosis. A triradiate pelvis, enlargement of costochondral junctions and bossing of the frontal and parietal bones are all features of osteomalacia.

19.5 **(A) 3075** **(B) 3075** **(C) 3075** **(D) 3075** **E 3075**
In the UK (though not in other European countries) Paget's disease occurs in about 3–4% of people aged over 40. Of these fewer than 5% have symptoms. In the past the incidence of osteosarcoma may have been overestimated; it probably occurs in 1% or less of those with symptoms. The humerus is the most common site for Paget's sarcoma. Deafness in Paget's disease is one of the most disabling symptoms and one of the most difficult to treat. It has many causes of which nerve compression is but one. Alkaline phosphatase is a good indicator of the status of Paget's disease; levels are high in severe disease and approximately related to radiological findings. Plasma acid phosphatase may be raised but is a better marker of metastatic cancer than of Paget's disease. Many patients with Paget's disease require no treatment.

19.6 **A 3079** **(B) 3079** **C 3079** **D 3079** **(E) 3079** ← true
Type I osteogenesis imperfecta is the most frequent form, accounting for about 60% of cases. Looser's zones are found in osteomalacia. There is an increased incidence of fractures of all bones, but especially the lower limb. Significant scoliosis is rare, unlike in types II and III osteogenesis imperfecta where the skeletal deformities are widespread. Both aortic incompetence and aortic root widening occur in oesteogenesis imperfecta. Blue sclerae is an important physical sign.

19.7 **A 3080** **(B) 3083** **C 3085** **(D) 3088** **E 3087**
Multisystem involvement including cardiac and cerebrovascular disease is a frequent finding in inherited skeletal abnormalities. Aortic incompetence,

aortic root widening and mitral valve prolapse are all common in osteogenesis imperfecta. Dilatation of the ascending aorta leading to aortic incompetence, and dissection, occurs in Marfan's syndrome. Thromboembolism can occur in any vessel and is the main cause of death in homocystinuria. Achondroplastic individuals show normal intelligence and no increase in cerebrovascular disease. Death is common late in childhood because of coronary artery disease in Hurler's syndrome.

SECTION 20: NEPHROLOGY

20.1 (A) **3102**   B **3102**   C **3103**   (D) **3103**   (E) **3104**
Detection of microalbuminuria requires a qualitative test kit. Gram-negative organisms will reduce nitrate to nitrites, which is detectable on multistix. Erythrocyte morphology can distinguish glomerular (>80% dysmorphic cells) from non-glomerular (<20% dysmorphic) haematuria. Tamm-Horsfall protein is secreted by the distal convoluted tubular cells and is the sole constituent of hyaline casts, which can occur in normal people.

20.2 A **3110**   (B) **3110**   C **3111**   (D) **3112**   (E) **3113**
Fatalities occurring with IVU are rare (1 in 100,000) and associated with arrhythmia and anaphylaxis. MRI, CT or Doppler ultrasound are preferred to renography for the diagnosis of renal vein thrombosis. MAG 3 and DMSA are both technetium-based but only the latter is avidly retained in tubular cells allowing assessment of scarring in reflux nephropathy. Captopril renography has higher sensitivity and specificity than IVU or IV-DSA in the detection of significant renal artery stenosis.

20.3 (A) **3121**   B **3121**   (C) **3121**   D **3121**   E **3121**
Patients with psychogenic polydipsia may drink up to 20 litres per day but plasma osmolality usually remains either slightly below or within the normal range. Nocturia is not a feature, due to the pattern of drinking and intact renal function. Dehydration tests (up to 5% loss of body weight), incorporating the use of intranasal desmopressin, allow differentiation between different causes of polyuria.

20.4 (A) **3140**   B **3140**   C **4141**   (D) **3141**   E **3142**
The anti-proteinuric effects of ACE inhibitors proportionately exceed any accompanying decline in renal function. Moderate salt restriction and

diuretics are the mainstay of treatment in nephrotic syndrome although abnormal water handling is observed. IgG provides the main defence against infection in tissues, but only children are particularly vulnerable to pneumococcus.

20.5 **A** **3150** **B** **3152** **(C)** **3162** **(D)** **3158** **(E)** **3158**
Microscopic haematuria is found at the outset in most cases of Henoch-Schönlein purpura and is the predominant renal manifestation of thin-membrane nephropathy, which may be familial, has a good prognosis and is associated with a basement membrane thickness of <300 nm. Goodpasture's syndrome is most often associated with acute renal failure and the nephritic syndrome, whereas a nephrotic presentation is commonest in MCGN.

20.6 **A** **3154** **(B)** **3156** **(C)** **3156** **D** **3156** **E** **3155**
Five per cent of children with minimal-change nephropathy continue to relapse in adult life. Highly selective proteinuria is seen in 75% of children but in less than 50% of adults. An increased incidence of HLA-DR7 or DR8 has been noted in patients with the condition.

20.7 **A** **3162** **B** **3162** **C** **3163** **D** **3165** **(E)** **3165**
Rapidly progressive glomerulonephritis occurs in Goodpasture's syndrome (where anti-GBM antibodies are pathogenic), SLE and is associated with ANCA positive vasculitis. Most patients require immunosuppression, and plasma exchange may also be beneficial. Renal transplantation can be successful provided autoantibodies are absent at the time of transplantation; they should also be monitored long-term.

20.8 **A** **3168** **(B)** **3168** **C** **3168** **(D)** **3171** **E** **3172**
The greatly increased relative risk of death in patients with diabetic nephropathy is due to cardiovascular disease. Diabetics constitute approximately 30% of patients on renal replacement therapy programmes but this figure may be greater in areas of higher ethnicity, where diabetic prevalence is increased. Control of hypertension, particularly with ACE inhibitors, has been shown to slow progression of diabetic nephropathy.

20.9 **A** **3175** **B** **3175** **C** **3175** **(D)** **3175** **E** **3178**
Staphylococcus epidermidis is the commonest infection of ventriculo-atrial shunts; mesangiocapillary glomerulonephritis (GN) may result. Prolifera-

tive glomerulonephritis (GN) may complicate salmonella infection, whereas the nephropathy associated with Legionnaire's disease is interstitial nephritis or acute tubular necrosis (ATN). Hanta virus is carried by rodents and leads to a form of haemorrhagic fever; the renal pathology is ATN and medullary haemorrhage. Chronic hepatitis B virus infection can induce membranous GN, hepatitis C a membranoproliferative GN associated with mixed essential cryoglobulinaemia, whereas nephropathy with hepatitis A is rare.

20.10 A 3214 (B) 3216 C 3217 D 3217 E 3219
Despite the introduction of new imaging techniques, such as radionuclide micturating cystography, standard micturating cystography remains the reference yardstick for diagnosis. DMSA scanning demonstrates focal scars more reliably than intravenous urogram. There is now evidence of familial occurrence of VUR such that screening of siblings and offspring is recommended, although no reliable genetic marker has been identified. Anti-reflux surgery is most beneficial to later renal function when undertaken early in infants with grades III–V reflux; in adults surgery can benefit patients experiencing loin pain associated with bladder distension or following micturition.

20.11 (A) 3222 B 3222 C 3223 (D) 3222 (E) 3222
In analgesic nephropathy a 'wavy' renal outline can be seen on intravenous urogram, and calyces are randomly affected; papillae may calcify and their necrosis is common. The condition predisposes to the development of urothelial malignancy, which is often multiple. The diagnosis can only be certain if the characteristic IVU findings are accompanied by a history of analgesic abuse.

20.12 A 3263 B 3266 C 3263 D 3263 E 3264
Gentamicin and tetracycline can both cause tubular proteinuria. Mild proteinuria is common with penicillamine therapy; nephrotic syndrome associated with membranous glomerulonephritis usually settles with withdrawal of the drug. Acute lithium toxicity may cause acute tubular necrosis, chronic intoxication and an interstitial fibrosis. Some patients with therapeutic lithium levels develop minimal-change nephrotic syndrome. Cisplatin is platinum-based and can lead to tubular proteinuria and tubulo-interstitial nephritis.

20.13 A 3270   (B) 3270   C 3274   (D) 3270   E 3274
Erythromycin and rifampicin both undergo hepatic elimination and should therefore not be affected by renal failure. Encephalopathy may result from high dose amoxycillin therapy in patients with advanced renal impairment. Oxypurinol, a metabolite of allopurinol, also accumulates and increases the likelihood of adverse effects such as bone marrow toxicity. Ranitidine is the preferred H_2-antagonist in severe renal failure. Although cimetidine is cleared by the liver its metabolites can lead to confusion.

20.14 A 3284   (B) 3282   (C) 3282   D 3284   E 3282
The sodium reabsorptive capacity is diminished (fractional sodium excretion >2%). In established acute tubular necrosis there is abnormality of urinary concentrating ability. The urine/plasma creatinine ratio is <20 and the urinary osmolality is <350 mOsmol/kg. Hypocalcaemia may rapidly develop as a result of hyperphosphataemia and disordered vitamin D metabolism.

20.15 (A) 3292   B 3292   (C) 3293   (D) 3293   (E) 3293
The histological appearances of myeloma kidney include typical fractured casts, tubular atrophy and multinucleate giant cells. Contrary to previous beliefs, patients with similar pathological immunoglobulin light chains may present totally different clinical pictures. Acute renal failure develops in 7% of patients with myeloma, and a higher proportion develop progressive renal failure; renal recovery is the exception rather than the rule. When the need for renal replacement ensues, a one-year survival of 50% may be expected.

20.16 (A) 3311   (B) 3311   C 3312   D 3307   E 3307
Relative contraindications to continuous ambulatory peritoneal dialysis (CAPD) include anuria (which impacts upon dialysis adequacy), severe inflammatory bowel or pulmonary disease and psychiatric ill health. Plasma proteins are regularly lost in peritoneal dialysis effluent and will exacerbate malnutrition. Recurrent herniae may make peritoneal dialysis impossible.

20.17 (A) 3314   B 3314   (C) 3314   (D) 3316   (E) 3316
Many patients receive a transplant during the pre-dialysis phase. Chronic severe infections preclude the immunosuppressive treatment necessary for

successful transplantation. Although amyloidosis is likely to recur within the graft it is not an absolute contraindication to transplantation. Allograft prognosis is improved by beneficial matching at the DR and B loci, but the induction of immune tolerance by deliberate previous transfusion is no longer widely practised.

20.18 A 3321 (B) 3321 (C) 3321 (D) 3321 E 3321
Erythrocytosis occurs in about 10% of patients and can be attenuated by ACE inhibitors, presumably by reducing erythropoietin production. The incidence is about 2% in the first year after transplantation, but squamous skin cancer is the most common malignancy. The excess cardiovascular risk seen in dialysis patients persists, and may even increase further, after transplantation.

20.19 (A) 3324 B 3324 C 3324 (D) 3324 E 3329
Osteomalacia and aluminium bone disease can only be accurately assessed by bone biopsy. Vascular calcification is common and accompanies elevation of the ionic production of calcium and phosphate (particularly when > 5.5). Severe hyperparathyroidism may respond to vitamin D therapy and appropriate metabolic control (of hyperphosphataemia and acidosis). Posttransplantation hypercalcaemia may result from persistence of hyperparathyroidism.

20.20 A 3323 (B) 3341 C 3340 D 3340 E 3340
'Classical' or distal renal tubular acidosis (RTA-1) is characterized by nephrocalcinosis and urinary stone formation, and may be inherited as an autosomal dominant. Hyperkalaemia occurs in RTA-4, and is related to aldosterone deficiency. RTA-2 can be associated with the Fanconi syndrome. The primary defect is failure to acidify urine, and the quantities of bicarbonate required to treat the acidosis are far less than in RTA-2, in which proximal tubular bicarbonate wasting occurs.

SECTION 21: STD

21.1 (A) 3346 B 3346 C 3347 D 3345 E 3348
In the UK non-specific and chlamydial infections are the most common STDs seen. The incidence of gonorrhoea fell in the 1980s with the appearance of AIDS, but this trend may now have begun to reverse. In the

UK the decline in syphilis has been maintained. There was an increase among males in the 1970s, particularly among homosexuals, but this trend has been reversed. The incidence of syphilis in women continued to fall during those years. The epidemiology of STDs in developing countries is very different from that in developed countries. For example they rank among the top five reasons for consulting doctors in many African countries, particularly in the 15–44 year age group. Trichomoniasis is the most common worldwide STD on the basis of WHO figures. In 1990 there were estimated to be 120 million cases. Heterosexual transmission of AIDS in developing countries predominates, perhaps because of the greater incidence of genital ulcer disease and also the relative scarcity of homosexuals in most populations.

21.2 A 3352   (B) 3352   (C) 3352   D 3352   (E) 3353
The first attack of genital herpes develops 2–14 days after exposure. Most attacks last about 20 days. Symptoms are more severe in women, in those never previously exposed to herpes simplex virus, and in men with anal herpes. The neonatal form is a devastating disease causing significant mortality and severe neurological complications in survivors. Recurrent attacks are usually shorter and less severe than the first attack, lasting on average about 7 days. Patients with a compromised immune system, for example those with HIV infection, may have longer, more severe recurrences.

21.3 (A) 3355   (B) 3355   (C) 3355   D 3355   (E) 3355
Bacterial vaginosis used to be known as non-specific vaginitis or gardnerella vaginitis, but it is now thought not to be caused by a single organism. Instead a change in the vaginal milieu allows colonization with a range of organisms including mycoplasmas, gardnerella and anaerobic bacteria. There is no inflammation of the bacterial wall (unlike in candidiasis and trichomoniasis) which explains the modern use of the term vaginosis rather than vaginitis. The common symptoms of bacterial vaginosis are vaginal discharge and an unpleasant odour (particularly after intercourse) but not pruritus. Metronidazole is the most commonly used antibiotic; clindamycin is also effective. Ampicillin or amoxycillin have only 50% efficacy while quinalones, tetracycline and erythromycin are ineffective. Recurrent attacks are common, perhaps because therapy is directed towards eliminating organisms rather than re-establishing the normal vaginal flora.

SECTION 22: BLOOD

22.1 **(A) 3404**   **B 3405**   **(C) 3406**   **(D) 3406**   **E 3409**
Acute myeloblastic anaemia occurs most commonly in elderly people; over 80% of patients are over 60 years old. The fact that it usually arises from a pluripotent stem cell is reflected by the occurrence of maturation arrest in the granulocyte, erythroid and megakaryocyte lineages in the different subtypes. Auer rods in circulating myeloblasts are diagnostic of AML but are only seen in about 25% of cases. The M3 promyelocytic type has the t(15;17) translocation and gives rise to problems with coagulation, frequently disseminated intravascular coagulation (DIC), for this reason it is important to identify it and also because of the use of all-trans retinoic acid in its treatment.

22.2 **(A) 3410**   **B 3410**   **C 3413**   **(D) 3413**   **(E) 3414**
The cure rate is approximately 70%, considering all children presenting with the disease. Although it is much more usual for individuals with Fanconi's to develop acute myeloid anaemia, they can instead get ALL. A much more frequent chromosomal abnormality predisposing to ALL is Down's syndrome. Around 2% of all children with ALL have Down's syndrome. The optimal period for continuing maintenance is not established, 2–3 years is probably best, and during this time co-trimoxazole is important prophylaxis against *Pneumocystis carinii*.

22.3 **(A) 3449**   **(B) 3450**   **C 3452**   **D 3452**   **(E) 3452**
PNH is a clonal disease, arising from a somatic mutation, and affects granulocyte, platelet and usually lymphocyte series as well as red cells. Haemoglobinuria secondary to intravascular haemolysis may be the presenting feature. Iron deficiency occurs because of chronic haemosiderinuria. Treatment is mainly supportive; the only definitive treatment is allogeneic bone marrow transplantation. Chemotherapy other than as conditioning for transplantation has no place.

22.4 **(A) 3470**   **(B) 3471**   **(C) 3471**   **(D) 3473**   **(E) 3474**
Approximately 60–70% of total body iron is present in haemoglobin, in health. Iron in vegetable foods is poorly absorbed compared with haem iron in the diet. There is no active excretion mechanism for iron, which is why iron overload states may need treatment with drugs to chelate excess iron.

Serum iron levels fluctuate widely, with diurnal and day-to-day variation in the same individual; it is not in isolation a reliable indicator. Serum ferritin is considerably more reliable and useful in most cases. Transferrin saturation has to fall to less than 16% before erythropoiesis is impaired.

22.5 **(A) 3477** **(B) 3478** **(C) 3479** **D 3479** **(E) 3579**
Although the male preponderance at presentation is 9:1, hereditary haemochromatosis is an autosomal recessive condition. Hypogonadism is usually hypogonadotrophic, i.e. due to damage to the hypothalamic-pituitary axis. Venesection should be energetic, and aimed to keep the Hb at about 12 g/dl. In recent series, hepatocellular carcinoma has proved the commonest cause of death, exceeding infection or cardiac or other chronic liver disease. In patients with thalassaemia major, desferrioxamine needs to be started after the patient has received 10–20 transfusions, usually around the age of 2 years. If the desferrioxamine is started years later, irreversible problems from iron overload may already be established.

22.6 **(A) 3489** **B 3489** **C 3490** **D 3491** **E 3496**
Parietal cell antibodies may occur in subjects with atrophic gastritis alone, but intrinsic factor antibodies are essentially specific for PA. Up to 35% of patients with HIV disease may have B12 deficiency, attributed to abnormal small intestinal flora.

22.7 **A 3502** **B 3502** **(C) 3503** **D 3504** **E 3510**
As alpha^0 thalassaemia trait is more common in SE Asia than elsewhere, it is frequently forgotten that beta thalassaemia occurs commonly in that region also, as well as in the Mediterranean, Indian and Pakistani populations more familiar to Western practitioners. The problem in the beta thalassaemia gene is usually a single base change or small deletion, in contrast to the alpha thalassaemia gene which is commonly deletional. The situation described in part E is haemoglobin H disease, which causes a moderate, usually well compensated haemolytic anaemia.

22.8 **(A) 3514** **B 3514** **(C) 3515** **D 3515** **E 3515**
A degree of jaundice is usual in people with sickle cell anaemia at all times, because of red cell breakdown and increased bilirubin production. The jaundice may become more marked during crisis. The spleen is commonly

enlarged in childhood but then is repeatedly scarred and usually shrinks to a size much smaller than normal, by the end of the first decade. Parvovirus (B19) may cause profound anaemia in any chronic haemolytic state. This occurs because of transient red cell aplasia – it is therefore an aplastic crisis.

22.9 **(A)** **3519** **B** **3519** **(C)** **3519** **D** **3519** **E** **3520**
The unstable haemoglobins result in haemolytic anaemia with detectable Heinz body intracellular inclusions; by contrast methaemoglobin arises when the haemoglobin molecule is oxidised to its Fe^{3+} form. Because of poor oxygen carriage and delivery by methaemoglobin, secondary polycythaemia might be expected but is uncommon in practice.

2.10 **A** **3521** **B** **3523** **C** **3522** **D** **3522** **(E)** **3523**
Primary acquired sideroblastic anaemia is a sub-type of the myelodysplastic syndromes, all of which can, to a greater or lesser extent depending on the type, evolve into acute myeloid leukaemia. Pyridoxine responsiveness is occasionally reported but is decidedly uncommon.

22.11 **(A)** **3526** **B** **3526** **(C)** **3527** **(D)** **3529** **E** **3529**
When red cells haemolyse and liberate haemoglobin, it binds to haptoglobin and the complex is removed from the circulation, and the level of haptoglobin falls. The half-life of Cr^{51} labelled cells is reduced in haemolysis from a normal value of 22–25 days. In hereditary spherocytosis it is the membrane associated proteins, ankyrin or Band-3 which are frequently defective.

22.12 **(A)** **3538** **B** **3538** **(C)** **3540** **D** **3540** **(E)** **3539**
Because of random X-chromosome inactivation (Lyon hypothesis) female carriers can be symptomatic, though usually less severely than affected males. The presentation in neonatal jaundice due to G6PD deficiency occurs at around 2–3 days old, not at birth, and the jaundice usually is more marked than the anaemia: these features contrast with those found in Rhesus incompatibility. Howell-Jolly bodies are a feature of asplenia, the denatured haemoglobin in G6PD deficiency can be demonstrated as Heinz bodies on supravital staining. Other features on Romanowski stain are poikilocytes and 'bite' cells.

22.13 **(A)** **3547** **B** **3548** **(C)** **3548** **D** **3549** **E** **3549**
In microangiopathic haemolysis a coagulation defect may occur depending

on the cause; those that give rise to disseminated intravascular coagulation (DIC) will be associated with coagulopathy, whereas in some other types, i.e. that due to cavernous haemangioma, no clotting complications occur. Spherocytes are usually seen as well as the characteristic red cell fragments. Rarely TTP may show some response to oral steroids, but in other clinical disorders associated with microangiopathy, steroids are unhelpful.

22.14 A 3551 (B) 3551 C 3552 D 3553 (E) 3554
In secondary polycythaemia, there is a true increase in red cell mass in response to another pathology, for example lung or renal disease. The polycythaemia attributed to reduced plasma volume is termed stress or relative polycythaemia. High affinity haemoglobin variants, which cause reduced oxygen delivery to the tissues, cause polycythaemia.

22.15 A 3556 (B) 3555 (C) 3557 D 3557 E 3556
Neutrophils and eosinophils are phagocytic, basophils are not. Neutrophils circulate for up to 12 hours, then migrate to the tissues and survive for a further 1–3 days. The finding of a neutrophil count below the 'normal' quoted for Caucasians, in people of black or Arab origins, is common. It is termed ethnic neutropenia, and unless there are any features associated to suggest another cause for the neutropenia, needs no investigation and is not associated with an increased risk of infection.

22.16 A 3562 B 3561 C 3562 D 3565 (E) 3568
Pain or tenderness in enlarged nodes frequently indicates an infective or inflammatory cause, but malignancy causing rapid enlargement may give the same features. Although Epstein–Barr virus infects B-cells, the node enlargement and peripheral blood appearances are due to T-cell proliferation attempting to eliminate infected B-cells. Non-Hodgkin's lymphoma is considerably more common than Hodgkin's disease by a factor of more than 3:1.

22.17 A 3570 (B) 3570 C 3570 D 3571 E 3571
Splenomegaly does not necessarily indicate true involvement with Hodgkin's disease. About 25% of patients have systemic symptoms at presentation. If disease is truly localized, local radiotherapy has a high chance of cure. The nodular sub-type of lymphocyte predominant Hodgkin's disease may relapse into large cell non-Hodgkin's lymphoma rather than recurrent Hodgkin's disease.

22.18 A 3572 (B) 3572 (C) 3572 D 3575 E 3575
Eosinophilia is sometimes present but is of no prognostic significance. A survival advantage in those patients whose staging has included laparotomy and splenectomy has not been demonstrated. Seventy to eighty per cent of patients survive to five years and there is a plateau after that time, so that many of these patients will have long-term cures.

22.19 A 3579 B 3580 C 3583 D 3585 E 3583
Gastric 'MALT'omas may be initiated by antigenic stimulus from *H. pylori*, and the lesions can regress if treated with suitable antibiotics. It is well recognized that the presence of systemic symptoms adversely affects prognosis in Hodgkin's disease, and the same is true of non-Hodgkin's lymphoma (NHL). There is a paradox in that low grade NHLs run an indolent course, whereas high grade tumours can be highly aggressive and have a very short prognosis if untreated. However, the high grade tumours have a higher true 'cure' rate, and cure of the low grade tumours is extremely difficult to achieve.

22.20 (A) 3588 B 3589 C 3589 D 3589 (E) 3590
The spleen contains a large amount of lymphoid tissue but the lymphocytes do not originate there, they migrate there from the bone marrow and thymus. The exact degree of enlargement needed to render the spleen palpable is variable according to body habitus but is usually 1.5–2 times normal, around 14 cm, would suffice.

22.21 (A) 3590 B 3590 C 3591 D 3591 E 3591
Hypersplenism can occur with quite modestly enlarged spleens, and conversely is not always seen when the spleen is massively enlarged. Splenic rupture can occur, uncommonly, in viral infections such as infectious mononucleosis, bacterial infections such as typhoid, and in haematological malignancies.

22.22 (A) 3597 B 3598 C 3598 D 3600 E 3601
The stage, Beta 2 microglobulin and albumin levels at presentation are among the important prognostic indicators. Interferon-alpha is the only agent which has been demonstrated to prolong plateau phase: it does so by an average of 6–9 months.

22.23 **(A) 3604** **(B) 3604** **C 3604** **D 3604** **(E) 3604**
Waldenstrom's accounts for a minority of patients with IgM paraprotein (less than 20% in one large series). Lymphocytosis can occur but is not common at presentation, it may occur late in the disease; lymphadenopathy is usually found at presentation. Bone lesions are not usually a feature of this condition.

22.24 **(A) 3630** **(B) 3631** **C 3631** **D 3631** **E 3631**
Although antibody binding to platelet surface antigens is the mechanism for thrombocytopenia in ITP, the normal life span of platelets is in the order of 10 days. Splenomegaly is not usually found at presentation; if present, a secondary cause for the low platelet count should be considered.

22.25 **A 3637** **B 3638** **(C) 3647** **D 3647** **(E) 3651**
The high spontaneous mutation rate is important because a negative family history does not exclude the diagnosis in a child with suggestive symptoms. The condition runs 'true' in kindreds, i.e. all affected males demonstrate a similar level of factor VIII:C deficiency. DDAVP is the treatment of choice in mild haemophilia and may be useful in some moderate cases too.

22.26 **A 3651** **(B) 3651** **C 3651** **D 3652** **E 3652**
Factor XI deficiency presents as a mild bleeding disorder, with few or no spontaneous haemorrhages, whereas factor VII deficiency can be as severe as classical haemophilia. Factor XII deficiency can predispose to thromboses due to deficient activation of fibrinolysis. A third of patients with severe factor V deficiency, unexpectedly, have a prolonged bleeding time; a test which is usually undertaken to demonstrate deficient or defective platelet function.

22.27 **(A) 3665** **B 3665** **(C) 3666** **D 3666** **E 3667**
Although the frequency of inherited problems in the natural anticoagulant system is increasingly recognized, acquired reasons for the problem (trauma, pregnancy, etc) remain much more common. The association between antithrombin III deficiency and arterial thromboses is not established; the deficiency usually causes predominantly venous events. The factor V mutation causing activated protein C resistance is now called factor V Leiden.

22.28 **A 3691 and 3692** **(B) 3692** **(C) 3692** **D 3692** **(E) 3690**
White cell depletion of red cells for transfusion does help avoid reaction due to HLA antibodies, but can much more easily be achieved by filtration through micropore filters, frequently now performed at the bedside at the time of transfusion. Haemoglobinuria especially is a feature of intravascular red cell destruction, due to transfusion of incompatible red cells, not to HLA antibodies which are chiefly directed at white cells in the product. Whereas major intravascular haemolysis should be avoided by meticulous cross-matching, it is certainly not possible to avoid all reactions in this way, e.g. those due to sub-detectable antibody as in delayed haemolytic transfusion reaction, due to HLA antibodies or plasma antibodies, nor those due to clerical or administrative error, e.g. administration of correctly cross-matched blood to the incorrect patient.

22.29 **A 3697** **(B) 3698** **C 3698** **(D) 3699** **E 3699**
T-cell depletion does decrease the incidence of graft versus host disease, but this is offset by an increase in the risk of graft rejection and leukaemic relapse. Fractionated total body irradiation does not give substantially better results than single dose total body irradiation, although it may reduce the risk of some long-term complications, e.g. sub-capsular cataracts.

SECTION 23: SKIN

23.1 **(A) 3706** **(B) 3706** **C 3706** **D 3706** **E 3704**
Skin colour is partly decided by the amount and activity of the melanocyte and partly by how much melanin is stored and processed in the keratinocyte. The melanocyte is found within the epidermis. Vasodilatation can increase the skin's blood flow by a factor of 100, making the skin well adapted for thermoregulation and wound repair. The epidermis is made up of stratified squamous epithelium comprising a germinative basal layer which sticks to the basement membrane. This layer generates successive layers of differentiating cells whose main function is to make the insoluble protein keratin. Epidermal cells turn over and die in a controlled way, the process taking about 30 days from the time of replication at the basal layer to loss from the surface.

23.2 **(A) 3713** **B 3713** **(C) 3713** **D 3713** **E 3713**
A macule is flat without change in surface marking or texture and may

consist merely of redness, purpura or melanin. A plaque is a disc-shaped lesion which often results as a consequence of coalescence of papules. Vesicles and bullae are both accumulations of fluid; vesicles being less than 1 cm in diameter and bullae more.

23.3 **A** 3716   **(B)** 3716   **C** 3716   **(D)** 3716   **E** 3716

Severe pain on compression of some masses is a well recognized symptom which aids diagnosis. If there is any doubt about the diagnosis, excision of the mass is recommended so that a definite histological diagnosis can be made.

23.4 **A** 3718   **(B)** 3718   **C** 3718   **(D)** 3718   **E** 3718

Each pregnancy has a 4% chance of giving rise to a congenital abnormality and during embryonic life maldevelopment can result in localized abnormal areas of skin. Most of these defects are not inherited although some are like the hypopigmented macule of tuberose sclerosis. Dupuytren's contracture is a thickening of the palmar, and occasionally plantar, fascia which has a familial incidence, particularly if it presents in younger patients. Accessory, fused or extra digits have a familial incidence too unlike accessory nipples which may occur along a line extending from the axilla to the groin which is the milk line of lower mammals.

23.5 **A** 3719   **(B)** 3719   **(C)** 3719   **D** 3719   **E** 3719

Knowledge about the genetic basis of disease is important because genetic counselling has become a key part of the advice doctors can offer. With most single-gene conditions, the risk of having another affected child is considerable – more than 1 in 10. With recessive heterozygotes one in four of the offspring will inherit the defect. There are other complications in that dominant, sex-linked or recessive forms of one condition may have distinctly different patterns of presentation and development. Thus, for example, the dominant form of ichthyosis is ichthyosis vulgaris which is distinct from the sex-linked ichthyosis seen only in males. The two 'false' conditions listed above, phenylketonuria and albinism, are both autosomal recessive conditions.

23.6 **A** 3723   **B** 3723   **(C)** 3723   **(D)** 3723   **E** 3723

Gastric atrophy and the presence of antibody to the parietal cell are associated with vitiligo and alopecia areata. Erythema nodosum occurs in a number of different conditions of which Crohn's disease is one; in Crohn's it may progress to pyoderma gangrenosum. Coeliac disease is associated with dermatitis herpetiformis, and gastric carcinoma with acanthosis nigricans. Pigmentation and malnutrition of the skin is particularly found in Whipple's disease.

23.7   A   3738   B   3736   (C)   3737   (D)   3737   E   3737
Certain metals, including nickel and chrome, have a greater affinity for the skin than others. This is thought to be partly due to their easier recognition and assimilation by the phagocytic Langerhans cells. Perfumes are a common cause of contact dermatitis, particularly those containing formaldehyde, tar and Dowicil. These ingredients may act as irritants as commonly as they do as allergens. Mercury is used for a great deal of dental work but not in the preparation of dentures. Rubber in the elastic of many garments may cause dermatitis but it is not used for making tights. Dermatitis may be caused by acrylic in spectacle frames, adhesive tape, dentures, hearing aids, artificial fingernails, sealants, printing plates and inks.

23.8   A   3744   B   3744   C   3744   D   3744   (E)   3744
Pruritus is the term used when the patient complains of itching but there is no obvious lesion to account for the symptom. It is induced by a number of agents including bradykinin, histamine, bile salts and proteases and potentiated by prostaglandin E. Iron deficiency is a recognized cause of pruritus, even when the patient is not anaemic. The iron deficiency may also cause thinning of the hair which can be a useful confirmatory sign. Acute renal failure does not cause pruritus, but in chronic pyelonephritis and chronic glomerulonephritis it is a prominent symptom. Haemodialysis does not necessarily remove it. The pruritus frequently found in polycythaemia is thought to be related to blood histamine levels and possibly iron deficiency. One in 10 patients with hyperthyroidism complains of pruritus, but itching is also common with the dry skin of hypothyroidism. Carcinoma of the lung is the cancer commonly associated with pruritus.

23.9   A   3746   (B)   3746   C   3746   (D)   3748   (E)   3748
The characteristic feature of psoriasis is a ten-fold increase in epidermal cell turnover. The cells pass rapidly upwards through the epidermis and seem not to have time to produce a horny layer. The cause is probably multifactorial. The lesion-free skin in affected people is not normal; psoriasis is

more readily induced and drugs such as chloroquine or practolol can quickly induce lesions in it. The Koebner phenomenon is the term used to describe psoriasis developing in traumatised skin. The incidence of polyarthritis in hospital patients with psoriasis is 7%. However, because both psoriasis and polyarthritis are common conditions there is a long standing debate about the link and there are those who believe it is a chance association. Local steroid creams are the treatment of first choice for many patients with a few plaques of psoriasis on the elbows, knees or scalp. About one-third of patients have their lesions controlled within 1–2 weeks by this treatment.

23.10 A 3751   (B) 3751   C 3751   D 3751   (E) 3751
The characteristic lesion of lichen planus is a shiny, flat-topped, violaceous papule. Histologically there is damage to the basal layer of the epidermis accompanied by an intense infiltration of lymphocytes plus a few histiocytes. The range of damage varies from extreme atrophy with ulceration and almost no epidermal cell turnover to considerable hypertrophy and hyperkeratinization resulting in thick nodules known as hypertrophic lichen planus. When the lesions heal they often leave pigmented rather than hypopigmented areas. Small white dots or lines may appear within the papules due to oedema, white cell infiltration and disturbance of vasculature. These are known as Wickham's striae. The destructive process can involve the hair follicle so that lichen planus is one cause of scarring alopecia. Telangiectasia is not a recognized feature.

23.11 (A) 3752   B 3752   C 3752   D 3752   E 3752
In acne there is an increase in the size but not the number of sebaceous glands. These large glands produce more sebum. They also produce more androgen metabolites which, in partnership with resistant bacteria, such as *Staphylococcus epidermis*, produce keratinization and hence blockage of the pilosebaceous ducts. The skin is a major site, along with the prostate and male genitalia, of androgenic conversion. Dihydrotestosterone is probably the end-organ effector.

23.12 A 3755   (B) 3756   (C) 3756   (D) 3756   E 3756
An association with other autoimmune diseases and a family history of such diseases is found in about one-third of cases of vitiligo. Associations include diabetes mellitus, pernicious anaemia, Addison's disease, myxoedema or thyrotoxicosis. The principal affected cell is the melanocyte which is

destroyed resulting in total depigmentation. The cause is unknown, perhaps an antibody or toxin not yet identified. The face and neck are usually affected early, followed by other sites such as axillary folds, in a characteristically symmetrical fashion. The depigmentation of vitiligo is usually total, although in early stages there may be hypopigmentation but such areas are never anaesthetic as in leprosy. Hyperpigmentation round the borders of the lesion is common.

23.13 A 3761   B 3761   C 3761   D 3761   (E) 3761
Up to about seven months of intra-uterine life the foetus is covered by long, soft hair. This lanugo hair is shed into the amniotic fluid. Hair growth occurs at the rate of about 1 cm per month but can speed or slow depending on circumstances. Eyelashes may lengthen in AIDS, malnutrition and chronic liver disease. A shock may cause premature moulting.

23.14 (A) 3770   (B) 3770   C 3771   D 3772   (E) 3772
Urticaria is a transient swelling and/or flushing of the skin mainly caused by mediators of inflammation acting on the small blood vessels. The knowledge that one of those mediators, histamine, plays a part in immediate-type hypersensitivity has caused the widespread misconception that all urticaria must be allergic. A non-immunological pharmacological explanation is likely in most cases. Familial urticaria is well recognized, including many large families with hereditary angioedema. Familial cold urticaria has been described in the USA. Food, medicines, infections such as *Candida albicans*, cold, heat and the sun are all known causes of chronic urticaria, but for most people the specific cause is never discovered. Although H_2-blockers have a theoretical role, they have not replaced H_1-blockers in the treatment of urticaria. The value of combined H_1- and H_2-blockers remains unproven.

23.15 A 3778   B 3778   (C) 3778   (D) 3778   E 3778
The pathogenesis of pyoderma gangrenosum is uncertain. It is not an infection but may be some sort of a reaction in which there is tissue necrosis, often with a heavy neutrophil infiltrate. Venous and capillary engorgement, haemorrhage and coagulation are prominent features. In many patients there may be evidence of a depressed immune status. The associated conditions include plasma cell dyscrasias and particularly myeloma. A bullous variety is associated with leukaemia, primary thrombocythaemia

and myelofibrosis. Common associations with Behçet's syndrome include thrombophlebitis, erythema nodosum, folliculitis and arthritis but not pyoderma gangrenosum. Rheumatoid arthritis, sero-negative arthritis with paraproteinaemia and Wegener's granulomatosis are known rheumatological associations.

SECTION 24: NEUROLOGY

24.1 (A) 3846 B 3846 C 3846 D 3846 E 3850
The localization of cognitive function regularly comes up in multiple choice examinations. Table I, page 3846, gives a clear summary. Hemineglect is a feature of parietal lobe lesions.

24.2 A 3866 B 3867 (C) 3869 (D) 3869 E 3869
Demyelination of the optic nerve is common in young people, associated with pain, especially on eye movement and may cause total visual loss. Asymmetrical chiasmic lesions cause unexpected field defects, see page 3868 of the *Oxford Textbook of Medicine*. Optic tract lesions are rare, the commonest being craniopharyngioma, pituitary adenoma and pituitary surgery. Damage to the optic radiation will cause a homonymous field defect (often asymmetrical); parietal lesions being inferior, temporal lesions superior (temporal at the top!). Prosopagnosia (the inability to recognize faces) is caused by bilateral occipital lesions as are cortical blindness and loss of colour vision (cerebral achromatopsia).

24.3 (A) 3871 (B) 3872 C 3872 D 3873 E 3873
The direction of nystagmus is specified by the fast phase and if to the right would suggest a right-sided cerebellar or brainstem lesion or left-sided vestibular lesion. Gaze evoked nystagmus is found in many conditions including pontine and cerebellar lesions and certain drugs especially anticonvulsants. Upbeat nystagmus is due to lesions at the level of the fourth ventricle and therefore may be associated with damage to the medial longitudinal bundle. Rotational nystagmus is rare but occurs with central lesions especially medial vestibular nucleus or cerebellar ectopia, hence the association with a syrinx.

24.4 (A) 3874 (B) 3874 (C) 3874 D 3875 (E) 3875
Seventy per cent of CPA tumours are Schwannomas (benign), therefore

radiotherapy plays little part in treatment, surgery is the only curative therapy. Neurofibromatosis type II is associated with acoustic neuromas (sometimes bilateral). Progressive hearing loss and balance problems are the most common presenting symptoms.

24.5　(A)　3877　　B　3877　　C　3877　　D　3877　　(E)　3877
Depression of the adducted eye is by the superior oblique muscle (trochlea, IV). The levator palpebrae contains some fibres innervated by the sympathetic nervous system (the muscle of Müller, hence partial ptosis in Horner's syndrome), the majority of fibres are innervated by the superior branch of the oculomotor nerve. The IIIrd, IVth and VIth plus upper division (Vi) of the trigeminal pass through the cavernous sinus (and also the superior orbital fissure). Anisocoria (unequal pupil size) is common in bilateral Argyll Robertson pupils. The skin over the angle of the jaw is supplied by the second cervical nerve root (C2) and not the trigeminal.

24.6　A　3878　　(B)　3878　　C　3878　　D　3878　　E　3878
Trigeminal neuralgia causes intense pain and may be seen in multiple sclerosis. There are many triggers including eating, therefore weight loss may develop. Carbamazepine is the treatment of choice and is usually effective at doses that do not cause significant side effects.

24.7　(A)　3884　　B　3884　　(C)　3884　　D　3884　　E　3884
Sinus arrhythmia is usually caused by vagal efferents decreasing their activity during inspiration, thus increasing the heart rate. Carotid sinus massage increases vagal activity therefore slowing heart rate. During the Valsalva manoeuvre, the blood pressure usually falls a little before sympathetic activity compensates by causing vasoconstriction, thus in a sympathetic lesion there is a continued fall of BP. Cocaine causes dilatation of a normal pupil and has no effect if there is sympathetic denervation. In contrast, methacholine has no effect on a normal pupil but causes constriction with parasympathetic denervation, as in the Holmes Aide pupil.

24.8　(A)　3892　　B　3893　　C　3893　　D　3893　　E　3894
The knee reflex is predominantly L4. SACD is characterized by degeneration of the cord, brain and peripheral nerves and may occur in the absence of anaemia despite severe disease. A syrinx causes loss of pain and temperature with preservation of vibration and joint position sense. A dorsal

column lesion causes the reverse. Note that both are dissociated. Neither should be confused with a Brown Séquard lesion in which there is preservation of all senses but dissociation between sides.

24.9 (A) 3911   B   3911   (C) 3911   D   3915   E   3924
The classification of epilepsy often causes confusion. Generalized seizures do not imply loss of consciousness merely whether EEG activity is widespread (generalized). Myoclonic jerks are generalized on the EEG as are absences. Tonic clonic seizures are generalized. However, they may be primary, or secondary to a partial seizure. Three per second activity is usually associated with typical absences and would mean loss of a driving licence regardless of the number of fits. The rules for driving and epilepsy were changed in 1994. A single seizure (even the first) means no driving for one year.

24. 10 A   3928   B   3927   C   3928   (D) 3928   (E) 3929
The driving licence may be withdrawn if there is excessive daytime sleepiness. Narcolepsy should be reported to the DVLC. Sleep paralysis occurs in about 15–20%, cataplexy in 66% and hypnagogic hallucinations in 35% whereas nearly all have excessive daytime sleepiness and the characteristic sleep attacks. Chlormipramine is sedative and therefore may worsen sleepiness, however it may abolish cataplexy and sleep paralysis. Amphetamines are used to treat the sleep attacks.

24.11 (A)   3947   B   3947   C   3947   (D) 3955   E   3956
The ophthalmic artery leaves the internal carotid artery before it branches into the anterior and middle cerebral arteries. The dura is supplied by both branches of the carotid artery and a lacunar infarct (small deep infarct usually in the basal ganglia, thalamus, internal capsule, cerebral peduncle or pons) may cause pure motor or sensory strokes as well as a mixed pattern or ataxic hemiparesis. A left hemisphere lesion may cause the head to turn to the left whereas a left brainstem lesion would turn the head to the right. A TACI is recognized as weakness of two or more body parts (leg, upper limb, face) with or without sensory signs plus homonymous hemianopia plus cerebral dysfunction (dysphasia, apraxia etc.) and is a result of infarction of the whole of the middle cerebral artery territory.

24.12 A   3965   (B)   3965   C   3965   D   3965   (E) 3967
Dementias may be divided into those with predominantly cortical disease
(Alzheimer's, CJD) and those with subcortical disease (most basal ganglia
diseases e.g. Huntington's, Parkinson's, Wilson's, see table 3 page 3967).
Cortical disease usually causes a disturbance of memory, language, praxis,
visuospatial and perceptual abilities whereas subcortical disease causes
disturbance of attention and executive functions (planning, problem solv-
ing) with slowing of responses but relatively preserved cortical function.

24.13 A   3964   B   3964   (C)   3964   (D)   3964   E   3964
Friedreich's ataxia is an autosomal recessive condition with onset in
childhood. There is degeneration of dorsal root ganglion cells, loss of
myelinated peripheral nerve fibres, degeneration of the dorsal columns and
Clarke's column, loss of fibres in the spinocerebellar and corticospinal
tracts. Nystagmus is present in about 25% of cases and pupillary reactions
are usually normal. There are associated skeletal abnormalities and T wave
inversion and ventricular hypertrophy in 70%.

24.14 A   3986   B   3987   (C)   3987   (D)   3987   E   3988
The gene for NF I is on 17, the gene for NF II on 22. Tuberous sclerosis is
inherited in a dominant fashion but most cases have no family history.
Depigmentation, adenoma sebaceum, multiple fibromas and a shagreen
patch are the skin manifestations and tuberous nodules of glial cells and
distorted neurones within the cortex may calcify. VHL disease is autosomal
dominant (chromosome 3) and is characterized by retinal angiomatous
vascular tumours and hemangioblastomas of the cerebellum or spinal cord.
Polycythaemia is the haematological abnormality. Ataxia telangiectasia is
inherited as an autosomal recessive condition and begins in early childhood.
Death usually occurs in the second decade.

24.15 (A)   3994   (B)   3994   C   3994   D   3994   (E) 3995
The onset of MS is characterized by a relapsing and remitting course in 80%
of patients. The remainder develop a progressive neurological dysfunction.
Benign disease is most common in young females. Pure sensory or optic
nerve lesions have a good prognosis. Motor involvement or coordination
problems have a poor prognosis as do patients with late onset disease (often
men). Oligoclonal bands in the CSF alone support the diagnosis of MS, if
they are also found in the serum, production within the CNS cannot be
implied.

24.16 **(A) 4008** **(B) 4008** **C 4008** **D 4008** **E 4008**
Wilson's disease (hepatolenticular degeneration) is associated with decreased ceruloplasmin in (95%) of patients. Presenting features would include jaundice, hepatitis, behavioural disturbance, tremors, dysarthria and drooling. A KF ring will almost always be present on slit lamp examination in the presence of neurological disease. The globus pallidus and putamen are collectively known as the lenticular nucleus (hence the term hepatolenticular degeneration).

24.17 **(A) 4024** **B 4024** **(C) 4024** **D 4025** **E 4025**
Migraine without aura (simple migraine) accounts for 70% of migraine. Migraine with aura (classical migraine) 25% and complicated migraine 5%. Complications such as hemiparesis are caused by vasoconstrictive ischaemia not emboli. Sumatriptan works almost exclusively on the blood vessels.

24.18 **A 4050** **B 4050** **C 4050** **D 4055** **E 4056**
Group B streptococcus, *E. coli.* and *Listeria monocytogenes* are the usual pathogens for most neonatal meningitis. *N. meningitidis, S. pneumoniae* and *H. influenzae* in children. *N. meningitidis* and *S. pneumoniae* cause 70–80% in adults. *H. influenzae* is decreasing due to the introduction of the Hib vaccination. A lymphocytosis may occur early in bacterial disease. Post-traumatic meningitis may be difficult to diagnose but should be treated as any community acquired meningitis.

24.19 **A 4075** **B 4076** **C 4076** **D 4078** **(E) 4080**
HIV disease causes many neurological problems either as a direct effect or as a consequence of reduced resistance to infection. The primary infection illness causes neurological problems in about 10%. Meningitis and encephalitis being the most common. During the asymptomatic phase, meningitis, polymyositis, neuropathy and cognitive dysfunction may develop. A neuropathy is present in 90% if investigated by neurophysiological methods. At the AIDS stage, HIV itself may cause severe damage to the cortical structures as well as muscle and nerve. Toxoplasmosis and cryptococcal infections are common and any bacterial, fungal or viral infection may occur. Primary CNS lymphomas may occur as may metastases from other tumours. Kaposi's sarcoma rarely metastasises to the CNS.

24.20 **(A)** **4096** **(B)** **4095** **C** **4094** **(D)** **4094** **(E)** **4094**
The dorsal branch of the ulnar nerve (sensory) leaves the ulnar nerve before the wrist. The median nerve supplies the pronator. The supinator is innervated by the deep branch of the radial nerve along with extensor digitorum, extensor digiti minimi and extensor carpi brevis. This branch then becomes the posterior interosseous nerve hence a posterior interosseous nerve lesion will not affect the extensor carpi ulnaris but will affect abductor pollicis longus, extensor pollicis longus and brevis along with extensor indicis. Although the radial nerve does not supply the muscles of grip, grip may be profoundly weakened in the presence of wrist extension weakness.

SECTION 25: DISORDERS OF THE VOLUNTARY MUSCLES

25.1 **A** **4145** **(B)** **4145** **C** **4145** **(D)** **4145** **E** **4145**
Duchenne muscular dystrophy (DMD) is an X-linked recessive condition. It therefore affects boys only since the gene is carried only on the X chromosome. Thus in X-linked disorders like DMD the females are carriers and the males suffer the disease. In DMD about one-third of cases are presumed to result from a new mutation in the ovarian cells of the mother or maternal grandmother. DMD usually becomes apparent in the third or fourth year with difficulty walking and climbing stairs and frequent falling. Most patients deteriorate steadily although some 'improvement' may be noticed between the ages of 5–8 when the rate of deterioration is outstripped by the rate of normal motor development. By the age of 10 most boys can no longer walk. High serum creatine kinase levels are characteristic of DMD and are found even at birth in children who will later develop the condition. Although some slowing of the rate of deterioration has been shown with treatment with steroids, most experts believe the side-effects outweigh the advantages and therefore do not recommend any specific treatment. The life-expectancy for DMD has improved in recent years due to preventative management, for example the prevention of scoliosis, and early treatment of complications, particularly respiratory infection and cardiac failure.

25.2 **(A)** **4152** **(B)** **4152** **C** **4152** **D** **4152** **E** **4152**
Muscle weakness and wasting rather than pseudohypertrophy are characteristic of dystrophia myotonia. Wasting of the masseters, temporal muscles and sternomastoids is almost invariable as well as forearm muscles (sparing the small muscles of the hands), the anterior tibial group, the calves and the

peronei. The muscle wasting appears to be due to a selective decrease in muscle protein synthesis. Cardiac conduction abnormalities and/or cardiomyopathy are common but the valves are spared. Ptosis is usual and ocular muscle involvement is common. Visual evoked potentials often show abnormalities of latency or amplitude bilaterally. Impotence is well recognized: the testes are small and histologically similar to Klinefelter's syndrome. Mental retardation is common as are some selective developmental cognitive defects. Progressive dementia was thought to be common but is now considered rare.

25.3 (A) **4161**   B **4160**   (C) **4160**   D **4161**   (E) **4162**

The most common presentations of myasthenia gravis (MG) are double vision and ptosis. Ocular symptoms occur in almost all patients at some stage of their life. MD is one of the best understood autoimmune diseases. The antigen is the acetylcholine receptor in muscle and the causative anti-acetylcholine receptor antibodies can be identified in about 85% of patients. The pituitary does not show histological changes. However, the thymus is often abnormal. MD patients under 40 years of age appear to be most prone to the thymic changes which include the development in the medulla of lymphoid follicles with germinal centres which are able to synthesize acetylcholine receptor antibodies. This may explain why thymectomy helps some patients. The characteristic feature of MD is painless weakness of skeletal muscle which worsens with exercise. Plasma exchange is a useful way of achieving short-term control of symptoms, for example during a myasthenic crisis or pre-thymectomy in weak patients.

SECTION 26: THE EYE

26.1 A **4180**   (B) **4180**   C **4180**   (D) **4180**   E **4180**

Conjunctivitis usually presents with redness of the conjunctiva, often affecting both eyes, and a sticky discharge of viral or bacterial origin. Episcleritis is a common complication of many systemic conditions and is not a threat to the sight, by contrast to scleritis which is a serious disorder and a threat to vision. Iritis presents with redness mostly round the cornea, pain, photophobia and corneal precipitates may be visible. Keratitis is associated particularly with herpes virus infection and some vasculitides, whereas rheumatoid arthritis is associated with scleritis. The pain in acute glaucoma may be very intense and vomiting is common.

26.2 **A 4186 (B) 4186 C 4187 (D) 4187 (E) 4187**
Glaucoma, hypertension, diabetes, some haematological disorders and occasionally systemic inflammatory disorders are risk factors for retinal vein occlusion. The onset of symptoms is not abrupt (by comparison with retinal artery occlusion) and may occur overnight. Thus the patient wakes with blurred vision which may develop into blindness. Retinal haemorrhages are the characteristic feature of retinal vein occlusion. If it is a central vein occlusion they occur throughout the fundus. With a branch occlusion a wedge-shaped area of haemorrhage appears in the area the vein drains with the apex of the wedge pointing to the optic disc. Improvement of the vision of the affected eye may occur. There are no studies of the benefit of long-term aspirin for retinal vein occlusion.

26.3 **A 4190 (B) 4182 C 4190 D 4190 (E) 4185**
Diabetes is a risk factor for cataract, accelerating development by an average of 5 years. Lens surgery is no different for diabetics and most diabetics are suitable for lens implantation, but postoperative complications occur more commonly. Uveitis occurs in systemic inflammatory disorders but not in diabetes particularly. Chronic glaucoma is more common in diabetics and measurement of eye pressure should be included in the screening programme for diabetic patients. Diabetics are prone to retinal vein occlusion and this should be taken into account should acute retinal haemorrhages occur. Episcleritis is common in patients with rheumatoid arthritis but diabetes is not a risk factor.

SECTION 27: PSYCHIATRY

27.1 **(A) 4204 B 4204 (C) 4204 D 4208 E 4208**
Approximately 20% of medical inpatients are found to have psychiatric disorders, most commonly depression, anxiety and alcohol dependency. These states have a significant influence on medical outcome through several routes (for example by poor treatment compliance) and hence prolong stay in hospital. The majority of patients suspected of having a depressive disorder should be treated by the medical team. Referral to a psychiatrist should be considered for patients with more severe illnesses or with failure to respond to an adequate treatment trial. Physical symptoms of anxiety are a common cause for presentation to physicians. It is unusual but recognized that severe mental illness may present with hypochondriacal complaints.

27.2 **(A) 4213** **B 4213** **(C) 4213** **(D) 4213** **E 4213**
There are two patterns of anorexia nervosa, restrictive and bulimic. In both types by definition weight is at least 15% below that expected for age, height and sex. In the bulimic type bingeing and purging are also features. Primary or secondary amenorrhoea due to low weight is a recognized presenting complaint. The majority of patients do not require naso-gastric feeding. This may be required occasionally with very severe weight loss and indicates a worse prognosis. There is no loss of secondary sexual characteristics. Head hair may be thin but pubic and axillary hair remain. Hypercortisolaemia does occur. Anorexia is a serious illness with a 25% mortality without treatment. With treatment the mortality is still 5%.

27.3 **(A) 4222** **(B) 4222** **C 4222** **(D) 4222** **(E) 4222**
He may have schizophrenia but there are many other more likely causes why a young man may isolate himself and his behaviour be described as odd. Social problems, drug abuse and depression should be considered. The majority of psychiatric patients are treated as outpatients. Even if he did require hospital treatment most admissions are as voluntary patients. The *Mental Health Act* is used when a patient refuses treatment and is thought to be suffering from a mental disorder of such severity that they are a risk to themselves or others. Hearing one's thoughts spoken out loud is a form of auditory hallucination and a first rank symptom of schizophrenia (third person hallucinations and running commentary are other auditory first rank symptoms). First rank symptoms at onset do not indicate prognosis. After a first episode 25% make a lasting recovery, 25% develop a chronic disorder and 50% have repeated episodes with varying recovery between illnesses.

27.4 **A 4216** **B 4216** **(C) 4216** **(D) 4216** **E 4216**
Many patients with BN have a past history of anorexia nervosa. Fluoxetine is an antidepressant and is effective in treating BN even in the absence of a clear depressive illness. Cognitive behaviour therapy is the treatment of choice for bulimia involving about 20 sessions over 5 months. Community surveys have found that 1–2% of young women have BN and most are not in treatment. Drug and alcohol abuse are a problem in a significant minority.

27.5 **A 4226** **(B) 4226** **C 4227** **D 4227** **(E) 4227**
Residual symptoms are more common in older patients. Elderly patients are more vulnerable to the side-effects of medication. A therapeutic dose for

elderly patients is within the same range as younger patients. Elderly patients with depression may seem cognitively impaired due to psychomotor retardation, apathy and poor concentration (depressive pseudodementia) which resolves once they are treated. Anxiety, agitation and irritability are characteristic of the elderly. Although a patient's illness may be understandable it still requires adequate treatment. Raised intracranial pressure is the only absolute contraindication to ECT.

27.6 **(A)** 4226 **(B)** 4226 **C** 4226 **(D)** 4226 **(E)** 4226
It is difficult to differentiate acute from chronic confusional states. Fluctuating level of consciousness is diagnostic of acute confusional states. Disturbed sleep patterns commonly occur in both acute and chronic confusional states. Having a past psychiatric history does not favour either diagnosis. Five per cent of the over 65s and 20% of the over 80s have Alzheimer's disease. Aggressive outbursts are uncommon and may occur in acute or chronic confusional states. Delirium tremens typically begins 48–72 hours after the last drink and is characterized by confusion, visual hallucinations, delusions, agitation, fear, autonomic overactivity and insomnia.

27.7 **(A)** 4230 **(B)** 4228 **C** 4228 **(D)** 4229 **(E)** 4228
If a patient urgently requires life saving medical treatment it can be given under Common Law. The physician has a 'duty of care' for that patient. The case may be discussed with a psychiatrist but the Mental Health Act refers only to treatments for mental disorders. Paracetamol and salicylates account for 30% of overdoses (minor tranquillizers/sedatives 15%, antidepressants 10%). DSH is more common in classes 4 and 5, urban areas and in young men and women. Personality disorder is found in 25–50% of cases. Psychotic illness is found in 12% of overdoses. Any chronic disabling illness is a risk factor for later suicide.

27.8 **(A)** 4248 **(B)** 4248 **(C)** 4248 **(D)** 4248 **(E)** 4248
All antidepressants should be continued for 6 months after recovery. Tricyclics are effective antidepressants and are often used in patients with suicidal ideation outside hospitals. Prescriptions for small numbers of tablets and close supervision reduce the risk of overdose. When the risk of suicide is high a safer compound may be used or hospital admission considered. Tricyclic antidepressants are used in all age groups although the

elderly are more sensitive to side-effects. Tricyclics are very effective anxiolytic drugs and do not have the same problems with tolerance, dependence and abuse which affect benzodiazepine use. Caution should be used when prescribing tricyclics to someone with ischaemic heart disease but they are only contraindicated in the case of either a recent myocardial infarction or with some cardiac arrhythmias especially heart block.

SECTION 28: ALCOHOL AND DRUGS

28.1   A   4272   (B)   4276   C   4277   (D)   4277   (E)   4277
The most useful biological markers of alcohol misuse are serum gamma-glutamyl transpeptidase levels and mean cell volume (MCV). The advantage of gamma-glutamyl transpeptidase is that changes in alcohol consumption are reflected in the serum levels within 2–4 weeks. Serum gamma-glutamyl transpeptidase levels are not a particularly useful screening test. Alcoholic coma has a mortality rate of up to 5% and admission to hospital is advised, particularly to monitor respiratory function. Wernicke's disease (or encephalopathy) is due to thiamine deficiency. The peripheral neuropathy of alcohol abuse is due to vitamin deficiency and chronic alcohol toxicity and is more common in lower limbs than upper limbs and only rarely affects cranial nerves.

28.2   A   4280   B   4280   (C)   4283   (D)   4283   E   4285
Ecstasy is the popular name for 3,4-methylene-dideoxymethamphetamine, which is a synthetic amphetamine derivative. Complications of misuse include hyperthermia, convulsions, collapse, disseminated intravascular coagulation, rhabdomyolysis and acute renal failure. Sudden death, particularly in children, from cardiac arrhythmias during an episode of glue sniffing are well recognized. Cardiac arrhythmias can also occur after cocaine use, even after apparently small doses, as well as other cardiovascular complications such as sinus tachycardia, ventricular tachycardia and even asystole. Heroin-related pulmonary oedema is the commonest cause of death in heroin addicts, often with the needle and syringe *in situ*. Candida infection in intravenous heroin users involves cutaneous, ocular, osteoarticular and pleuropulmonary involvement.

28.3   (A)   4290   B   4290   (C)   4290   D   4290   E   4290
Tachycardia is characteristic of the alcohol withdrawal syndrome but not

atrial fibrillation. Perceptual changes which may occur include hallucinations, often auditory and usually voices, as well as hyperacusis. Jaundice is not a feature of alcohol withdrawal in most cases. Severe alcohol dependence, simultaneous misuse of sedative drugs or a previous susceptibility may cause the development of grand mal fits on withdrawal. Three to four fits may occur over the first 12–24 hours of withdrawal but progression to established epilepsy is rare.

SECTION 29: FORENSIC MEDICINE

29.1 **(A) 4310   B 4310   C 4310   D 4310   (E) 4310**

It is a requirement to report a death to the coroner during an operation or before recovery from an anaesthetic. This means all deaths 'on the table' are mandatory and also deaths within 24 hours of an operation. Most coroners would not regard such a report as mandatory for patients who died within a year of an operation unless the death was thought to be due to the surgical procedure. A death from occupational disease or poisoning should automatically be reported to the coroner. Any death in which the cause of death is unknown should be reported to the coroner, and similarly if the deceased was not seen immediately after death. Only a tiny minority of deceased patients are not seen after death and it may soon become law, like other countries, that they are. There is no particular requirement for patients with AIDS to be reported to the coroner unless there is doubt about the diagnosis or suspicious circumstances.

29.2 **(A) 4311   B 4311   C 4311   (D) 4311   E 4311**

The diagnostic tests for brain stem death should be made by two doctors and repeated once. The absence of spontaneous respiratory movements is an important criteria but it must be in the presence of a high PCO_2. Fixed, unresponsive pupils, absent corneal reflexes, absent motor responses in cranial nerves and an absent gag reflex are all important criteria. The persistence or otherwise of spinal reflexes is not relevant in the diagnosis of brain stem death.

SECTION 30: SPORTS MEDICINE

30.1 **A 4321   B 4321   C 4321   (D) 4321   (E) 4321**

Exercise ECGs are the most useful diagnostic tool in middle-aged men who wish, for example, to start exercise training and who may have a strong family history of coronary disease, strongly positive risk factors for coronary disease (for example, smoking), symptoms suggestive of myocardial ischaemia or a history of exercise-induced syncope. Asymptomatic men with an abnormal exercise ECG are 10–20 times more likely to develop coronary disease than the general population. On the other hand, over 70% of asymptomatic men with abnormal exercise ECGs will have arteriographically normal coronary arteries and will not develop overt coronary disease within five years, so there is a significant false positive rate. There is about one death for every 3,000 exercise ECGs performed and clearly those with angina are at greater risk. However there is no reason to avoid exercise ECGS in people with angina provided all parties are aware of the risks and sensible precautions, such as the availability of cardiac resuscitation equipment, are taken. Exercise ECGs are not generally recommended as a screening test for asymptomatic men wanting to exercise. To postpone the death of one asymptomatic middle-aged jogger, 15,000 tests would have to be performed.

30.2 **A** 4323 **B** 4323 **C** 4323 **(D)** 4323 **(E)** 4323
X-rays of stress fractures may appear normal at first; later they may show callus formation. A simple bedside test is the sharp pain produced at the fracture site by insonation with a physiotherapist's ultrasound applicator. This test is particularly useful in distinguishing between a tibial stress fracture and medial shin soreness. Bone scintography is the best diagnostic test available. The second and third metatarsals are the most commonly affected bones in the foot. Plaster of Paris casting is rarely required for stress fractures. Weight-bearing should be avoided if painful and all sports which might stress the fracture should be avoided.

30.3 **(A)** 4325 **(B)** 4325 **(C)** 4325 **D** 4325 **E** 4325
The adult liver usually stores about 100 g of glycogen and 350 g of muscle. Sugar or glucose consumption just before endurance exercise is not recommended because it suppresses fatty acid mobilization and so speeds muscle glycogen depletion. The higher the concentration of carbohydrate in an ingested fluid, the slower the stomach empties, so ingesting a fluid containing high concentrations of glucose may be counter-productive. During a marathon glycogen stores become depleted and the runner becomes increasingly dependent upon fatty acid mobilization for fuel.

SECTION 31: MEDICINE IN OLD AGE

31.1 **(A) 4334** **B 4334** **(C) 4334** **(D) 4335** **E 4335**
The normal values for coagulation tests persist into old age. There is a slight
fall in haemoglobin concentration, affecting women more than men so that
by the age of 75 a haemoglobin concentration in the range of 11.5 to 11.9
g/dl should not necessarily be interpreted as anaemia. There is a decrease
in the elasticity of the aorta and its main branches, often accompanied by an
increase in their diameter and length. The cardiac output has long been
thought to fall with age but recent work has suggested it does not. In older
age there is a rise in residual lung volume but total lung volume stays the
same.

31.2 **A 4336** **(B) 4336** **(C) 4337** **(D) 4337** **E 4338**
Inappropriate prescribing and the adverse effects (which increase in old age)
of some drugs cause about 10% of admissions to hospitals of elderly people.
Drug absorption generally varies little with age. In old age the glomerular
filtration rate falls and so does the elimination of drugs by renal tubular
secretion, for example, penicillin and aminoglycosides. The effect of
warfarin on the synthesis of clotting factors is increased in elderly people.
The administration of thiazide diuretics to elderly people is a significant
cause of potassium depletion, particularly as they often eat a comparatively
low potassium diet. So potassium supplements or alternatively potassium-
sparing combination drugs are required.

31.3 **(A) 4341** **(B) 4341** **C 4342** **(D) 4342** **E 4342**
Cardiac pain in elderly people is often slight and may well be overshadowed
by other symptoms such as confusion. Cardiac infarction may even be pain
free. Basal lung crepitations are found in many elderly people without a
specific aetiology being identified and are thus not diagnostic of heart failure
on their own. Digitalis is indicated in patients with atrial fibrillation (AF)
and an uncontrolled ventricular response as well as in those with AF and
a slow ventricular rate. It is important to check renal function in all
digitalized patients and to match the dose to function. ACE inhibitors are
valuable in treating heart failure symptomatically, particularly the fatigue,
and in reducing mortality.

SECTION 32: TERMINAL CARE

32.1 **(A) 4351   B 4351   (C) 4351   D 4352   E 4355**

Hyperalimentation, either enteral or parenteral, has not increased survival in advanced cancer patients and is not appropriate for terminally ill people. Corticosteroids in low dosage usually lead to an improvement in appetite within a week. High-dose progestogens have also been shown to improve appetite and reduce weight loss, but they should be reserved for patients who fail to respond to corticosteroids. Most chronic cancer pain is nociceptive, caused by mechanical stimuli in affected organs and conducted along intact somatosensory pathways. A proportion is neuropathic, caused by damage to the central or peripheral nervous system. Eighty per cent of patients with bony metastases gain significant pain relief from a single treatment with radiotherapy. Haloperidol is usually effective in treating uraemic vomiting, but sometimes the sedating phenothiazine, methotrimeprazine is needed.

32.2 **(A) 4352   (B) 4352   (C) 4352   (D) 4352   (E) 4352**

Morphine can be given orally because it is well absorbed, mainly in the proximal small bowel. Morphine's active ingredient, morphine-6-glucuronide, passes comparatively slowly through the blood–brain barrier, which probably explains why isolated doses of morphine have poor results compared with repeated administration. Diamorphine is identical in action to morphine and no more effective for severe pain. The plasma half-life of morphine is about 3 hours, so morphine should be given 4-hourly. Epidural injection is given 12 hourly or by infusion and is not associated with neuropathic leg pain. It is most useful when oral morphine causes unacceptable side-effects.

INDEX

PASTEST REVISION BOOKS AND COURSES

PasTest has been established in the field of postgraduate medical education since 1972, providing revision books, practice exams and intensive revision courses for doctors preparing for professional examinations.

PasTest Intensive Revision Courses are run before each examination at convenient locations in major cities. All courses offer top quality revision materials and expert teaching.

PasTest Practice Exams and Revision Books are available for MRCP Parts 1 & 2 (General Medicine, Paediatric & Clinical), MRCGP, DRCOG, MRCOG, DCH, FRCS, FRCA, PLAB & undergraduate finals.

The following books, published by PasTest, contain useful revision material for doctors studying for the Royal College of Physicians MRCP Part 1 examination and for other medical examinations containing Multiple Choice Questions.

	ISBN
MRCP Part 1 MCQ Revision Book	0 906896 86 X
MRCP Part 1 Practice Exams	0 906896 49 5
MRCP Part 1 MCQs with Subject Summaries	0 906896 55 X
Explanations to the RCP Green Book	0 906896 57 6
Medicine International MCQ Book 3	0 906896 65 7
Medicine International MCQ Book 4	0 906896 87 8
MRCP Part 1 MCQ Pocket Books	
1: Cardiology & Respiratory Medicine	0 906896 18 5
2: Neurology & Psychiatry	0 906896 19 3
3: Gastro, Endo & Renal Medicine	0 906896 23 1
4: Rheum, Haem & Infectious Diseases	0 906896 24 X

For a full catalogue of current titles, courses and prices please contact
PasTest, Dept. OTM, Freepost, Knutsford, Cheshire WA16 7BR
Tel: 01565 755226   Fax: 01565 650264